BACK FROM THE ABYSS

The Autobiography of a
LOW-BOTTOM ALKY

BY KIERAN DOHERTY

Published by:
Cap & Bells Press
New York City, New York

www.capandbellspress.com

Be the first to receive exclusive information on
new releases and authors from Cap & Bells Press.

Visit www.capandbellspress.com to sign up for our mailing list.

Contents

Foreword

By Mark Morgan Ford

In 1982, I was 32 years old. I had just taken a job as the editorial director of a newsletter publishing company in Boca Raton, Florida. We used freelance writers regularly and I needed to hire another one right away.

I interviewed a handful of recent college graduates… and then Kieran Doherty appeared in my office. He looked romantically scruffy in a tweed jacket (with elbow patches), a button-down Oxford blue shirt, and a knit tie. His pants were corduroy. He wore desert boots.

He was older than the other candidates by more than 20 years. His face was handsome in a rugged, Irish sort of way. He had red hair and expressive brown eyes.

"I'm ready to work," he said as soon as he sat down. His voice had a pleasing craggy tone.

I looked at his resume. Lots of experience as a newspaper reporter and columnist.

"Why would you be interested in writing newsletters when you have so much experience with newspapers?" I asked. "It seems like a step down."

"Newspapers don't pay very well," he said. "And I need a job."

I had turned down an offer with *The St. Petersburg Times* to take my job with the newsletter publisher, so I was curious about the life of a newspaperman. I asked Kieran what it was like. He told me a few stories that made me think I'd made a mistake in turning down my offer.

"Sounds pretty exciting," I said.

"The salary you are offering sounds exciting to me," he replied.

"Doherty," I said. "That's an Irish name."

He looked at me guardedly.

"I'm Irish myself," I said, feeling foolish.

"So what do you do when you're not working?"

"What is this?" he said. "A job interview or dial-a-date?"

And then he smiled. He had an irresistible smile.

I laughed. We talked about being Irish-American. We talked about his interests. He liked classical music and Irish history and he owned a wooden sailboat he had been restoring for some time. In his spare time, he was working on a novel, he said.

"Aren't we all?" I said.

"So," he said. "Can I call you boss?"

I told him about the job, the workload, and deadlines, making it sound as formidable as I could.

"I'm your man," he said.

He was a great hire. His writing was smart and clean, requiring little editing, and he made all his deadlines. We worked together for six months. One day, after he had completed an especially difficult assignment, I gave him a bonus of 500 dollars in cash. I told him about a full-time position that was opening up in our editorial department. I said I thought he could do it, and that it would make me very happy to have him working full-time for us. He thanked me and promised to give me an answer the following Monday.

He didn't show up on Monday... nor did he on Tuesday... nor did he the rest of the week. Phone calls to his apartment went unreturned. I asked my assistant to try to track him down. I even suggested she check with the county to see if he had been reported dead or missing. There was no trace of him.

Several months later, out of the blue, he walked into my office, sat down, and said, "Remember me?"

His clothes were dirty. He needed a shave. He looked like he had been dragged through a briar patch.

"Where the hell have you been?" I asked.

"Do you really want to know?"

"I do."

"I will tell you the truth," he said. "But you won't like it."

"Try me."

He was, he said, grateful for the bonus and the job opportunity.

"With the newspaper industry in decline," he said, "I could see that I had a good future with you. I realized you were offering me a better life — and that may have been what scared me."

He told me that, on his way home, the cash I had given him was "burning a hole" in his pocket.

"So I did something I shouldn't have done," he said. "I stopped at a little bar about a block from my apartment and ordered a drink."

He paused, clearly expecting a reaction.

"And so?" I said.

"Well, I guess I never told you that I'm a low-bottom alky."

"Low-bottom alky. What does that mean?"

"I'm a drunk," he replied. "A bona fide alcoholic."

I told him I didn't believe in alcoholism. "It's just a euphemism for drinking too much," I said.

He roared with laughter.

"Hey," I said. "I like to get drunk now and then. But I don't call myself a drunk."

I talked him into meeting me for breakfast every week or two at The Green Owl, a greasy spoon on Atlantic Avenue in Delray Beach.

I am not sure why I pushed for this. I suppose it had something to do with the fact that I felt I didn't spend enough time with my mother when she was dying of Lou Gehrig's disease.

I expected our first meeting to be difficult. Kieran was dying. Dying is something we all must experience, but it is also, at least in my mind, the worst of all human experiences.

What could I say to him?

Among his other admirable qualities, Kieran was not a Pollyanna. And he didn't tolerate the warm and fuzzies. So feeding him words of encouragement or denial was out.

He was already seated at a small table when I walked in. He smiled at me as I sat down. I still didn't know what to say but I knew I had to look him in the eyes.

"It sucks," I said.

"Tell me about it."

The waitress came over to take what was to become our "regular" order for the next two years. Two fried eggs — over easy for me, sunny side up for Kieran — whole-wheat toast, and coffee.

I asked him for details about his prognosis.

"It's not good," he said.

The cancer was already well-developed. The doctors at the veteran's hospital were recommending a pretty standard course of chemotherapy and radiation, but they did not suggest there was much chance of a recovery.

I encouraged Kieran to seek other opinions — even alternative therapies — but he was not comfortable with that. He seemed resigned to following the conventional protocols.

Having been involved with the publication of alternative health newsletters for many years, I was convinced he was making a mistake. I pressed him until he agreed to try some natural remedies once the chemotherapy and radiation were concluded.

The next time we met was shortly after his first treatment. He looked a bit tired — but other than that, none the worse for it. I asked him how he was doing. He said something like, "I'm still here." I asked about Lynne. She was fine, he said.

We began again to talk about what a shitty thing it was to have a terminal disease. All our conversations, I felt, were going to be going in this direction because… what else could be on his mind?

"I suppose I shouldn't complain," he said. "After all, I've lived a full life."

I had known Kieran long enough to have picked up lots of the bits and pieces. To say that he had lived a full life was hardly an exaggeration. I told him I thought his story should be a book. "It could be a big seller," I said. "What you've been through borders on the unbelievable."

He laughed. I told him I was serious.

"I don't think I'll have the energy," he said. "Besides, the only thing I'd be interested in writing would be that novel I've been talking about for years."

"Well," I said, "I can help you. You can fictionalize your experiences and start to write them up as your novel. Meanwhile, when we get together, you'll tell me your story, beginning at the beginning. I'll record what you say and use that information to fill in any holes."

He thought about it for a minute and then said, "Okay. Let's give it a try. "

The next time we met, he looked stronger. He handed me the first chapter of his novel. "Tell me if you think this is worth pursuing."

I took out my tape recorder and put it on the table. He eyed it suspiciously. "What's that?"

"I told you," I said. "You're going to tell me your story and I'm going to record it."

"I forgot about that," he said. "I don't think I want you to do it."

"Why?" I asked.

"Because the real story might hurt too many people."

"Don't be ridiculous," I said. "It's your life. You lived it. You had some tough years, but that's over… you made it… what's to be ashamed of?"

"Plenty," he said.

And then he started talking.

PROLOGUE

Take Them Clothes Off, Boy!

A cold day 30 years ago.

I sat near the back of an unheated Bluebird bus as it turned down a narrow country road about 10 miles north of Gainesville, Florida. I stretched my neck to see past the bulk of the brown-uniformed driver. Through the streaked window, I saw the prison a half-mile ahead.

"There it is," someone in front of me said.

There it was. Lake Butler Correctional Institution, the maximum security prison that would be my home for the next three years. I'd expected to see something more sinister. Some mammoth, gothic structure with battlements and ramparts. Instead, it looked like a rural junior college campus, a cluster of one- and two-story houses and several larger buildings that could have been dorms.

But then I saw the soaring double chain link fence, topped by rolls of razor wire that ran around the complex. And the gun towers, manned by two men with automatic weapons. Ready to shoot.

It was grim but I wanted in. It was bone-aching cold on the bus and my summer clothes (which I'd had on when I was arrested more than six months earlier) were not enough to keep me warm. My hands were swollen and tingled from the tightness of the handcuffs. I'd complained about them, but the two uniformed guards who sat behind the driver and in front of a security gate had just smirked.

The bus sighed to a stop. I looked out my window but all I could see was the fence, the base of one gun tower, and the side of what I later learned was the prison administration building.

The driver honked the horn. I heard the grating, mechanical sound of a large gate opening. The bus inched its way toward the building and then stopped.

"Bus in! Close the sally port!" someone shouted.

For long moments the bus sat idling. Then the guards stood up from their seats and descended from the bus without so much as glancing back to where we sat. The doors closed. I could hear them talking to other guards but I could not make out what they were saying. There was a good deal of laughter.

After what seemed like an hour, a tall, lanky guard climbed on board. He wore a 10-gallon hat. His uniform was spotless and iron-creased. The tips of his cowboy boots were spit polished. The only thing lacking was a pair of mirrored sunglasses, but he compensated for that by holding a toothpick between his teeth.

"My name is Cellblock Slim," he said, and then grinned, briefly. "You may have heard of me."

There were about 20 of us on the bus, mostly tough-looking blacks and Latinos. This was a maximum security state prison, and the crew I was part of looked like it, along with Cellblock Slim, had been chosen by some B-movie casting director.

In answer to Slim's comment, several of my fellow convicts nodded. This wasn't their first trip to Butler.

But it was mine and I felt — to put it mildly — out of place. It was like the beginning of a Rambo movie, with me cast as Woody Allen.

My throat was dry and my chest was pounding. I wanted a drink. A good, hard drink. If not that, a cigarette.

But there would be no drinks for me here.

"My job is to keep you in line," Slim said. "And I promise you I'll do that."

"You see that fence," he said. "It's not there to keep you in. Me and my boys will keep you in. That fence there is to keep the good people outside, the people you have robbed and raped and whose families you've murdered, from coming inside and giving you what you deserve. So be thankful for that fence. And worry about me."

Then he walked up and down the aisle between us. He took time to look us each in the eyes directly. The toothpick shifted from the right side of his mouth to the left.

"I don't give a shit if you like me or not," he continued. "But you damn well better hope that I like you. Because if I *don't* like you, I goddamn guarantee you I will make your life inside fucking miserable."

Then he flashed that grin again. A black guy across from me mumbled some profanity under his breath. Slim walked over to him slowly, stopped, and pulled a club from his belt. He pointed the end of it at the man's chest and leaned on it.

"You are new here, aren't you?"

The man said nothing.

"Yes, I know you are new. And you probably think that when you get inside this fence you will be in a bad place."

He leaned harder on the club. The man glared at him. "But inside this place there is another place that is twice as bad. And inside that bad place there is another."

Now he pushed so hard on the club that the man groaned.

"I already think I don't like you, pal. You better start thinking about how you can change my mind."

"What a crock," I thought. "This guy's been watching too many bad movies. He's full of shit."

Soon enough, I found out that Slim wasn't full of shit. At Butler, there was no limit to his ability to act upon his threats, as twisted and melodramatic as they sounded.

"Off the bus!" Slim shouted.

With that, the double doors at the rear of the bus swung open. Outside stood two guards, their arms crossed, gesturing with their heads for us to hurry up.

"Line up and strip!" Slim shouted. "Empty your pockets. Stack your clothes at your feet with your other belongings on top of the stack!"

Slim and his two assistants moved from man to man, unlocking handcuffs.

"Get them clothes off, boy!" they snarled. "And them filthy underwears too!"

We did as we were told, some looking like they had been through this drill many times before. Then we stood there naked, hands over our genitals, looking straight ahead for fear of being spied on or spying or who knows what.

For maybe four hours, we stood there, shivering in a narrow corridor between the two chain link fences.

Did I say it was November? It was late November. And if you don't know Florida, you might think the weather in late November is very nice. Well, maybe it is in Miami. But not in Butler, where afternoon temperatures can drop to 40 degrees and feel much colder with the wind blowing from the north at 20 miles an hour. It was fucking freezing.

The guards moved away from us and huddled. They drank coffee and read magazines. I had no idea what we were waiting for. It was turning into night and the weather was only getting worse.

If it weren't for the fact that I was surrounded by men whom I had already come to fear, I would have broken down and cried. I would have.

"What am I doing here?" I kept thinking. "I'm not a criminal. I'm an honest man. I'm a father and a husband and a freaking newspaper editor, for Christ's sake."

I just couldn't believe it. I promised myself that I would remember this day forever. "As long as you live," I told myself.

And then I had a consoling thought, which almost made me smile. "Well, at least things can't get any worse."

Man, was I ever wrong.

The Baby Store

The way I like to imagine it, my parents saw me first in a glass display box, one of a row of such boxes, each containing a baby in need of a home. There I lay, wrinkled and pink, about the size of a fryer chicken, my mouth wide open and screaming for air.

I picture Dad in a fedora, holding Mom's elbow as they look from box to box. Mom's lips are pursed, Dad's brow wrinkled in thought. She leans in for a closer look.

Let's take him, she says. *Let's take this one!*

I was born on March 2, 1945, the bastard son of a French-American girl named Rose Menier, who died seconds after I clawed out of her womb and into the glare of an operating room at the University of Chicago hospital on the city's south side. My father was a soldier who left his girlfriend to fight one of the last battles of World War II. I want to believe that he loved my mother and died not knowing he'd left behind a son. I imagine him as a brave man, perhaps a heroic one like the dogfaces you see in the movies. When I think about it, which is not often, I picture him dying with a bloodstained picture of my mother in his hand.

I see my mother as a fine and sensitive girl, an incurable romantic who gave her virginity to her soldier boyfriend the night before he sailed off to his fate in the Pacific.

That is what I like to imagine. What I actually know is my mother's name and the date and location of my birth.

I know too that I was baptized within minutes of my birth. And that I was delivered premature, blue and squealing. I weighed less than three pounds, and was kept in an incubator at the hospital for a month. That's when my adoptive parents, Mary and Patrick Doherty, took me as their child.

I like the idea that I was picked out like a Sunday roast or a Thanksgiving pumpkin. In reality, my adoption was arranged by a priest friend of my parents who felt sorry for the tiny orphan who was expected to die before his first birthday.

My parents wanted to name me Columbanus in honor of the sainted Irish monk. They reconsidered, my mother told me, when their priest friend suggested that the baby in the incubator had enough problems without getting stuck with Columbanus. And so they called me Kieran.

When my parents took me home, I was so small that my father could hold me in one of his big, callused hands. My first crib was the second drawer of my parents' clothes bureau.

"The doctors didn't think you would live," my mother told me many times. "But you did."

I was the second baby adopted by my parents who thought, mistakenly, they could never have children of their own. Kevin, my older brother, had been adopted two years before me. Then, two years after my adoption, my mother got pregnant and had their third son, who was named Patrick after my dad.

Growing up, I never felt that I was anything other than my parents' child. I had no sense that I didn't belong or was an outsider in my family. I had no idea, in fact, that I was adopted until I was 9 or 10 years old. I remember the day vividly. My parents took me aside and showed me the adoption papers. My mother told me what she knew of my biological mother.

"We've always loved you as our own," my mother said as my father nodded in agreement. Never once did I doubt it.

Still, I was plagued by a feeling of apartness. It was as if there was a subtle but discernable wall between me and everybody else. Years later, in acting school, I was told I had a "director eye." It had something to do with remaining detached from the action on stage, of never allowing myself to be pulled into a scene.

In truth, I have never felt entirely part of any scene I was in, on stage or in life. I've always felt like I was floating over the action, observing and unobserved. Perhaps that's why my favorite moments were when I was alone, playing games I invented in my bedroom, daydreaming or reading in a wingback chair in the living room.

One day when I was a young man, acting in an amateur theater production in Clearwater, Florida, I received a telephone call from a woman who identified herself only as Mrs. Clark. She spoke so softly I could barely hear her.

"I had a son," she said, "a baby boy I had to give up for adoption."

I felt the hair on my arms and the back of my neck rise.

"I never saw him again," she said, "but when I saw you on stage last night, I thought I'd be happy if he grew up to be like you."

I thanked the woman and hung up the phone. I hadn't told her I was adopted, but wished I had. I also wished I'd told her that I was drunk during the play and had no recollection of what I'd done on stage. And that my marriage was on the rocks... that I was cheating on my wife... and that I was desperately unhappy and didn't know why.

"You wouldn't be happy if your boy was like me," I should have told her.

Or maybe I'd be happy if I was like him, as she imagined him to be.

Secrets and Silences

My dad was a Tipperary man. Growing up, he could look out his bedroom window and see the tumbled ruins of the round tower and Cormac's Chapel and the other medieval buildings atop the Rock of Cashel.

He'd climbed that mountain — said to be the spot where St. Patrick converted the King of Munster 15 centuries ago. Back then, he never dreamed he'd leave his home and that craggy mountain behind. Yet he did, and stayed away for almost 50 years, almost long enough to forget the mountain's silhouette against the sky.

In many ways, my father was a shadow man, a man of secrets, of silences, abetted in his secret-keeping by my mother. I know almost nothing true about his life in Ireland or his early years in America.

For years, I thought my father grew up in a thatched roof cottage with a dirt floor and no plumbing. I imagined him and the rest of the clan crouched around the hearth eating potatoes and nothing else and damn few of those.

In fact, the family home was a two-story Georgian number, blue with white trim and a commode that leaked but flushed and even a bathtub and shower. The farm was small, but large enough to warrant the hiring of the village idiot to help with the heavy lifting.

It wasn't that my old man was a liar. Or rather, he didn't lie for any benefit, other than the relief that comes with not having to face the truth. And so, to tell his story, I find myself half-lying, mixing guesses with the little bit I know for sure.

He did not often speak of his childhood, or of his early years in America; hardly ever let on how he felt; was undemonstrative. When I think of him, which I do often, I think about how hard he worked throughout his life.

Like many Irish men of his time, he was shaped by want and labor, first by the ubiquitous poverty of Ireland and then by the Great Depression in America. Eventually, he was able to put aside some money and enjoy some prosperity in the later years of his life.

"Talk is cheap," he'd say. "It takes money to buy whiskey."

He believed that the world was a hard place and that success was had by hard work and sometimes aggression. "You've got to stick it to the other guy before he sticks it to you," he'd say, thrusting his hand forward and twisting it as if it held a knife.

He didn't say whether he was happy with what he'd accomplished. "All I want," he'd say, "is for my sons to do better than me."

He was the middle son of three boys — as I am. His older brother Willie stood to inherit the family farm in the Irish way. That left my father, Patrick, and the youngest boy, John, to build a future for themselves.

By the time my father celebrated his fifth birthday, his father, John Doherty, was dead. The old man's photo, the one I've seen, shows a rakish young man wearing a derby and a high, stiff collar. His handlebar mustache, thick and black, shines, its ends pointed sharp as needles. He seems to be daring the photographer to say something out of line.

The family story was that my grandfather died at the hands of the British. In fact, he died of a heart attack, leaving behind a wife with a thirst for porter and three sons too young to care for themselves.

Like many men of his generation, my father resented the British for the suffering that began under Queen Elizabeth I and continued under Cromwell and during the Great Famine and in Churchill's early days. This resentment colored his thoughts throughout his life and, although I don't like to think so, probably colored my own.

Born in 1905, my father was 11 when Padraig Pearse and his fellows lost their lives taking control of the General Post Office (GPO) in Dublin. He was a teenager during the Irish Civil War and was affected by its many privations and abuses.

Tipperary was a hotbed of Irish Republican Brotherhood at that time, so it is not surprising that my father's family was supportive of the cause. It's not clear just what happened, but my father and his brothers fell afoul of the law. The family story — and this is probably true — is that the family home was used as a safe house by rebels on the run from the English and later the Black and Tans.

The three boys were arrested. John was about 15 at the time. Young and powerless, they could easily have disappeared into the bowels of the English prison system and never been seen again. Instead, a family friend with political clout somehow gained their freedom after three months.

My father didn't talk much about his time behind bars but he did tell me that there was a proposal for a hunger strike by some of the older rebels in the jail. "I didn't want to starve and yet I couldn't vote against it. So I prayed that the vote would fail. I promised God that if I survived I'd go to mass and Communion every day for the rest of my life."

He survived but he didn't keep his promise.

After getting out of jail, my father and my Uncle John decided to flee Ireland. The alternative — living the rest of their lives looking over their shoulders — was not appealing. And so they went to the one place on earth where an Irishman could hide: England.

It was not a pretty life in England. My father and uncle had to eke out a living in the black market, always fearful they would be found out.

Later, many years later, when my father and mother owned a little motel in Florida, I saw just how great his anti-British feelings were. It was summer, the time of year when the motel was always nearly empty and every guest was treated like a king. Four tourists dropped in and wanted to rent two rooms. My dad was all sweetness and blarney, lathering them up with a brogue thick enough to cloy. The tourists filled out a registration card and slid it across the desk. Dad looked at it.

"Oh," he said, "you're from London."

"Yes," one of them answered.

"I'm sorry," he said, shaking his head. "We have no vacancies."

If my grandfather was a shadowy figure, he stands solid as stone next to the ephemeral memory of my grandmother Kate. My father never mentioned her name in my presence, as far as I recall.

"Your father and his mother didn't get along," my mother explained. "She was a woman who made bad choices."

Some terrible choices they must have been, for my father never returned to Ireland despite the urging of his older brother Willie. He refused to make peace with her even as she lay dying in a bedroom at the top of the stairs in the ancestral home.

If my dad and I had enjoyed something like a normal relationship when I was a young adult, maybe we'd have talked about his mother and what had passed. But by the time I was old enough to ask him meaningful questions, we were separated by a river of booze.

It was not until after my dad's death that I learned that Kate Doherty was herself a secret drinker who'd almost lost the family farm. The drink was delivered to her door each evening in exchange for a growing mountain of IOUs. At the time of her death in the 1960s, my dad had to help Willie pay her outstanding bar tab or the house and farm would have been taken.

Sometime in the late 1920s, long before Kate's death, my father and his brother John traveled together to Canada, and from there to Boston. The No-Irish-Need-Apply signs were no longer on display in Beantown, but jobs were as scarce as hens' teeth. So my father and uncle traveled on to Chicago, where some other Tipperary men had settled.

John started his life in America roaming from job to job. And after he married and lost his wife, he began to drink heavily and live on the fringes of society, as I would later do.

My dad took a different path. He worked as a maintenance man at a Catholic church, a charity job, then as a butcher for Harding's Corn Beef, swinging a boning knife sharp as a razor. He ultimately used his gift of gab and soft Irish brogue to parlay that entree into a full-time job as a salesman, peddling corned beef to Irish taverns.

What a job that was! The taverns gave away free sandwiches with their beer, and treated him to both when he came in. A job with free eats and drinks plus a paycheck was perfect for my dad at the time. He was a hard worker and an ambitious soul, but he was also tight as the bark on a tree.

On a lark one day, he went to a church carnival. Walking along, not paying attention to where he was going, he bumped into a red-haired girl, Mary Molloy, who had just come from a fortune-teller's tent where, the story goes, she was told that she'd marry a dark-haired man from across the seas.

Soon enough, the fortune-teller's words came true. They were married, and my father went to work for his father-in-law, Mike Molloy, the president of the Grain Trimmer's Local Union.

He worked as a grain-trimmer, spending long days shoveling soybeans and wheat and barley in the great elevators along the Chicago River or deep in the dusty holds of riverboats.

He often left the house before sunrise to attend an early church service, then drove his old car through the gloomy landscape of South Chicago to his job. He'd come home late in the day, park the car in the garage behind the four-flat he and my mother had bought as an investment, get out of his work clothes in the basement, and climb the stairs to their apartment.

I remember greeting him when he came home from work. I remember the hallway that led to the basement door, and the basement with the coal bin and furnace and one wooden wall hung with tools and, for some reason, a golf bag holding a few rusted clubs. I remember taking comfort in the smell of the grain dust in his hair and clothes and the Lucky Strikes he smoked but always managed to put aside for Lent.

I remember, too, my fifth birthday, when he greeted me in that hallway wearing a voluminous pea coat. Smiling, he reached into one of his deep pockets and pulled out a trembling, black and white ball of fur. It was a puppy he'd found on an Alaskan cargo ship. I named it Pal in honor of the dog that played in the pages of some picture book I happened to be reading at the time. No matter that the dog was a female. Pal was the name I wanted and the name that little girl-puppy got.

My father was not an emotionally demonstrative man. I don't remember being held on his lap or carried piggyback or embraced. He showed his love in other ways.

"Your father works very hard to take care of us," my mother said frequently. Or "Don't make noise, your dad works very hard and needs his sleep."

On weekends and days off and even late on summer evenings when the fireflies gathered to twitch in the bushes, he puttered around the yard. He seemed to love working on the building's front door. Brass-hinged and brass-knobbed, it shone in the sun. The colored glass windows on either side glistened, and still he polished and polished.

Sometimes, after hours of mowing the tiny front lawn and trimming the boxwood hedges and sweeping up the sidewalk, he'd take us to Cunis's ice cream shop on 79th Street, just a few blocks away. We'd get cones that made our hands all sticky as we marched home, Kevin and Pat and me in front, pushing and punching; Mom and Dad behind, not holding hands but talking, always talking.

My dad was a workingman, but he was no drunken lout of a shanty Irishman so popular in fiction and so prevalent in fact. We were Lace Curtain and proud of it. We boys were taught to keep family business within the family, to talk softly in public, and to make sure our underwear was clean, just in case we were hit by a trolley car. We didn't have much money and we didn't have a coat of arms hanging in the front hallway that proved we were descended from a king who ruled from Tara's throne, but we had class, such as it was.

By the time of my First Communion, my grandfather had retired and my father had taken over as the president of the local longshoreman's union. His work load eased a bit then, and so we were able to have dinner together as a family.

We were expected to show up for the meal with clean faces and hands, to say grace and to eat what was put before us. We had roast beef every Sunday, meatballs and tomato gravy every Wednesday, macaroni and cheese and fish sticks on Friday, steak on Saturday. If I were somehow transported back in time to that childhood dinner table, I'd know just what day of the week it was by the food being served.

Though he had little formal education, my father was a serious reader. He read Aquinas, Thomas More, and other great writers who were represented in the blue volumes of the Harvard Classics collection that lined one of the bookcases in the front room.

Discussions at our dinner table were about politics and ideas, with my parents doing most of the talking and the three of us, Kevin, Pat, and I, doing a lot of listening or looking as if we were listening.

Some of my fondest memories of those days are of my dad teaching me how to use a paintbrush and how to splice an electrical cord and even how to plane down a sticky wooden window so it would slide easily in its tracks. "These are skills that last a man a lifetime," he'd say.

Not a Moment Too Soon

When I heard about my father's death, I laughed. Not at first. My first reaction was a loss of breath. Not because the announcement was unexpected. He was 89 years old. He'd suffered two heart attacks already.

"Dad is dead," my younger brother, the lawyer, said over the telephone. "Heart attack." His voice was small.

It was later, hearing the details from my mother that the laugh came.

He died doing what he most loved to do, and he said then just about exactly what I figured he'd say, exactly what I hoped to say when I died.

It was St. Valentine's Day in 1994. A bad storm had come through the day before, knocking palm fronds and leaves across the lawn outside my parents' home in Florida. Even after two heart attacks and a bypass operation, my father didn't let himself slow down much, so he'd been clearing debris off the lawn all morning, reaching high overhead with a trimming saw to get the fronds that dangled broken.

At lunchtime he came in, removed his shoes as he always did, and stood at the sink swallowing the pills my mother had him take at every meal. He sat down at the table and he and my mother ate lunch together, talking about the work he had done and was going to do. My mother said he seemed happy.

As he bent over to put on his shoes, he suddenly straightened up, grabbing his chest. He looked surprised, my mother said. "Not frightened," she said. "Surprised."

By the time the paramedics arrived, my mother thought he was dead. But they found a pulse and began working on him. After a few minutes, my mother told them to stop. "I was afraid they'd bring him back as a vegetable," she said.

My father had made it very clear that he didn't want to live his last days hooked to "some damn machine." But he had also said, "Don't let me go one minute too soon."

"I think that was exactly the right time," my mother said. "Not a moment too late but not a moment too soon."

"Did he say anything?" I asked.

"Oh, shit!" she said. "Those were his final words."

That's when I laughed. My old man. Working till the end. Enjoying a meal with his Mary. And then cursing his luck.

and lived a better life than my father could have imagined when he was sitting in a pony cart in Ireland. Our family wasn't wealthy, by any means, but there was always food on the table.

If there was a problem — and it would have been a problem for an Irish Catholic couple — it was that my mother could not get pregnant. And so, with the help of a family friend who happened to be the head of Catholic Charities in Chicago, they adopted a bouncing baby boy they named Kevin Joseph. Two years later, they adopted me, a sickly, premature little bundle of trouble, not expected to live, but named Kieran Joseph. Two years after that, when I was growing fat and starting to talk, my mother and father had a biological child, Patrick Desmond.

I remember sitting on the floor in our kitchen, on the tile under the fold-down ironing board that my mother lowered every Saturday afternoon. The radio, as it always was on those afternoons, was tuned to the Texaco-sponsored broadcast of the Metropolitan Opera in New York and my mother was singing, not very well. I grew up listening to *La Boheme* and *Turandot* and *Carmen* and *The Marriage of Figaro*, sitting on the cold floor at her feet, staying still because she wanted me to and because I wanted to be close to her.

Not long before she died, I watched mother watching Pavarotti on television singing "Nessun Dorma," our favorite aria. She'd pulled her chair as close to the screen as she could and was leaning forward intently, gazing at Pavarotti's face. As the tenor sang, her lips moved silently in tandem with his, singing the words to herself.

My mother was both soft and hard. Soft when she could afford to be and hard when she had to be. I've seen her cry after nearly running over a little boy who had darted into the street in front her car, then storm up to the front door of the house where the child lived and raise hell with his mother for not watching him.

She had a look when she was angry that made her daunting to children and to most adults.

Once she had a disagreement with a storeowner about a television we'd purchased that never quite worked properly. After several fruitless attempts to get him to repair it or refund her money, my mother — with me chugging along manfully behind her — entered the store at a time when she knew he would be busy with customers. Charging up to him, her heels rat-a-tat-tatting like machine gun fire, she started complaining, at the top of her voice, about the miserable service she'd received, about how many trips she'd made to the store only to be disappointed, about how much money we'd spent there, and about how she'd never again buy so much as a toothpick from him. Shaking her finger in the owner's face, she continued her tirade until his half-dozen or so would-be customers had scooted out. Then she stopped and fixed that look of hers on him. We left that day with a brand-new TV.

My mother is as responsible as anyone for turning me into a writer. She got me interested in books cleverly, by starting me off with exciting stories and then gradually leading me to more challenging fare. In those early years, I read the Landmark "You Were There" series and the entire cycle of Oz stories. She bought me *A Child's Garden of Verses* one week when I was out of school with a cold, and introduced me to the *Knights of the Round Table* and John Hawkins and *The Count of Monte Cristo*.

Later, after I'd won a citywide writing contest in the fifth grade, she told me I could be a poet or a novelist or a journalist if I wished — and then she challenged me to read widely. When I was 11, I read *Gone With the Wind* cover-to-cover in the back seat of the family car as we drove from Chicago to Florida. I became familiar with the character of Holden Caulfield long before I was old enough to appreciate him. I flipped through *The New Yorker* every week in search of articles and stories I could understand.

"You can do anything you want," she said more than once. "But if you want to be a writer, be the best writer you can be."

I don't think I became the best writer I could be. A life not very well lived got in the way. But I did become a writer, earning a living by putting words on paper. Eventually, I had a dozen books published, and dedicated more than one of them to her.

My mother worked as hard as her husband, not shoveling grain but taking care of her family. She washed clothes every Monday, when washing clothes meant rubbing them against a ribbed washboard before throwing them into a stand-up washer, wringing them out, toting them to the backyard to pin them to a drooping clothesline, and folding them when they were dry. She ironed and swept and vacuumed and scrubbed. She cooked, like most Irish, not well but dutifully.

She dealt with the tenants who rented apartments in our four-flat and com-plained about the plumbing or the windows sticking or just for the hell of it. She carried garbage cans downstairs when she had to and shoveled coal more than once to keep the apartments warm in winter. She didn't mind shoveling snow, either, though she drew the line at mowing the lawn. At the end of the day, she'd sit with my father in the living room, her feet up, sipping a glass of tawny Port.

When we were all in school and the apartment was empty during the day, she began filling in as a substitute teacher. For the next 20-odd years, she taught, upgrading her college degree after we moved to Florida to become a school librarian. I don't think her students loved her. She wasn't that kind of teacher. But they respected her, I'll bet. I'll bet they knew when she walked into a classroom or the library that she meant business. When she told them to be quiet, I know they listened. And I'm certain they learned.

Sometimes she and my father would fight. These fights often broke out on Saturday nights, after we'd spent the evening at our grandfather's house, watching television with Uncle Kevin and Grandaunt Na. There'd be high-balls for Mom and Dad and beer for Uncle Kevin, even sherry for the old lady, so the fights probably had something to do with the drinking.

When they fought, we stayed well out of their way, in our bedrooms all the way at the rear of the apartment. On occasion, I'd hear indistinct shouts and, less frequently, crockery breaking. Once, there was the dull sound of what I later learned was a silver candelabra as it bounced off the wall.

They fought over money and other matters that couples usually fight about — though I never heard enough to really know what had set them off. Some-times, when I believed they were fighting about me, I'd kneel beside my bed and put my hands over my ears to make sure I couldn't hear their words.

In the morning, the crockery was always swept up, the trouble over — or so it was meant to seem.

Of all my memories of my mother, my fondest is of us going to church to-gether, not on Sundays but on those early weekday mornings when it was my job to serve as an altar boy for the earliest mass.

As we walked along the still-dark street, moving from one white circle cast by a streetlamp to the next, she'd slow her pace so I could stay at her side and hold her hand. Then I'd serve mass for old Father Howard, who had a terrible problem with gas and farted each time he bent his head over the missal or the altar, even the host. I'd fight not to laugh and say a prayer, which was never answered, for God to make the poor man stop farting, not for his sake but mine. At Communion, I'd hold the golden paten under my mother's chin, and after the priest slid the host into her mouth, she'd wink. On the way home, I'd feel her presence as a comfort, knowing that all was right in my world, at least for that day.

That Little Shit Sammy

Shortly after my fifth birthday, I started kindergarten at Our Lady of Peace Elementary School, just a few blocks from our apartment in South Shore. I was several months too young to begin school officially, but Mother had already taught me the basics of reading and writing — and armed with those skills, and her adamancy, I was allowed to attend classes.

O.L.P. — that was how we referred to the school — was housed in a squat, two-story building that looked more like a factory than a place of learning. It was part of a complex that included the parish church, the convent, the rectory, and an asphalt-covered playground that served as a parking lot on Sundays.

Conceiving of this space as a playground demanded religious faith, as it contained no swings, no slides or sandboxes — nothing, in fact, that could be used in play. Its only notable feature was a painted yellow line that split it in two, the line that separated the boys from the girls. And that separation was enforced with the same seriousness as the Line of Demarcation drawn by Pope Alexander VI in 1493 that divided the world into two halves, one owned by Spain, the other by Portugal.

The school itself was also divided by gender, since it was assumed that mixing boys and girls together, as was done in public schools, would lead to sin.

We wore uniforms. Long-sleeved blue shirts, with blue ties, embroidered with the cursive letters "OLP." No jeans allowed. Most boys — and I was one of them — wore wide-wale corduroys that whispered with a "zwoop-zwoop" sound when the legs rubbed together. And a group of boys clad in these trousers and walking down the hall together emitted a chorus of noises like those a flock of parakeets might make if they were trying to pass themselves off as barn owls.

We were taught by Dominican nuns — stern, haughty women in white habits and black cloaks, huge rosaries draped at their waists. What hair they had was hidden by a wimple and veil arrangement that looked tight and uncomfortable. There was a rumor that the sisters (that's what we called them) were bald beneath their headdresses, and that their pates were kept shaved clean by Gus the barber, in his shop, on Wednesdays when he was "closed."

I have no specific memories of going to that school except one. In class one day, the teacher, Sister Mary Something, told us to draw a familiar object and then to print the object's name below the drawing. I drew a box with windows and wheels, my rendering of a city bus like those that ran up and down 79th Street and along Jeffrey Avenue, a block from where we lived. I painstakingly wrote a few words under the picture and handed it to the nun.

The next day, our pictures were hung around the room, taped to the wall. Sammy Ross, a small, black-haired kind of impish boy, pointed at my picture and laughed.

"Look at what Kieran wrote!" he cried.

He pointed to the sentence I'd painstakingly scrawled beneath my drawing: "This is a bus and it rides on people."

The class laughed and my face burned. I wanted to run from the room and hide. I didn't recognize it at the time, of course, but I was very sensitive to what others thought of me. Much later I would come to realize that I would do almost anything — cheat, steal, tell any lie, play any role, give up pieces of myself without even thinking — in order not to feel the way I did that day.

The fear of this feeling fueled my drinking in bars from Tokyo to Tijuana, on dance floors, in newspaper offices, in bedrooms and marriages.

It's been almost 60 years since Sammy Ross made the class laugh at me, and I still haven't forgiven the little shit.

In the fellowship of sober alcoholics that I'm in, it's suggested, strongly, that we get rid of resentments we have, including those that stem from our childhood. We're told that if we don't find a way to forgive our former enemies or transgressors, we will turn our anger against ourselves and begin drinking again. I am sure there is great wisdom in that advice — and, in fact, it has helped me stay sober. But I think I will go to my grave still angry at Sammy Ross.

The Grocery Store Heist

It's been a while since I've stolen anything. Years, in fact. That may not impress some, but to me it's an achievement. I spent most of my life stealing pretty much anything that wasn't nailed down. I was never a big-time thief, more of a minor-leaguer. But I stole.

I stole from my parents. I stole from friends. I stole from my grandfather. I even stole from school. It wasn't that I needed any of it. It was just that I wanted to get away with it.

At first, it was a thrill. Then, it became a habit. Eventually, that habit bit me in the ass.

I was seven years old when I pulled off my first heist. Like all my subsequent thefts, it was poorly planned and executed. I walked the five blocks from our apartment to the Kroger grocery store on 79th Street. I wore my baggiest pants, fitted with deep pockets.

In the store, I searched out the least-used cash register. I waited until no shoppers were in the register line and then crawled like a crab into the empty space in front of the candy display. Shaking with excitement, I grabbed handfuls of candy and stuffed them into my pockets. Then I strode nervously toward the front door. Just as I approached it, I heard the cry:

"Hey, you! Hey, boy!"

I turned and saw a man, stout and balding, bearing down on me like a middle linebacker. I bolted. I ran down 79th Street, skid around a corner, and galloped along a side street. Looking over my shoulder, I saw the linebacker galloping after me.

I sped up, confident I could outrun him, but my heavily laden pockets made it difficult. Realizing that I needed to lighten my load, I pulled candy bars, bags of M&Ms, jawbreakers, and licorice from my pockets as I raced across the front lawns that lined the street.

Looking over my shoulder again, I saw that I was pulling further and further away from my pursuer. Feeling safe, I slowed to a trot. Then, suddenly, I tripped over a small hedge and went ass over teakettle. Even before I stopped tumbling, I was in the sweaty grip of the panting mammoth.

He dragged me back to the store, seated me on a folding chair in the manager's office, and left the room. For at least an hour, the manager grilled me. What's your name? Where do you live? What are your parents' names?

Luckily, I was prepared for this. I stayed staunchly silent, just like the POWs I had seen so many times on screen at the Avalon. My interrogator might have been a Japanese torturer. He could not break my spirit. I was even threatened with jail. Nothing worked. I would not give up my secrets.

I did give him a name but it wasn't mine. And when he said, "How do you think your parents will feel when they find out about this?" I told him they were the one's who'd put me up to it.

"Dad is out of work and Mom is crippled," I said. "Every morning they send me out to steal candy so the family will have something to eat."

"Mom's waiting at home for me now," I said. "If I don't come back with some candy, I don't know what she will do!"

The store manager looked at me with incredulity. "Are you telling the truth?" he asked. I put my hand to my heart and swore "on my dead sister's grave."

I could hardly believe it myself, but his eyes softened. He put his hand on my shoulder and squeezed gently. "Poor kid," he said. And then he let me go.

I was as proud as I imagined Dillinger was after a successful bank job. I ran home laughing, loving my freedom. I threw open the front door and bounded up the stairs. At the top of the landing my mother stood, waiting for me. I could see by her expression that disaster had reasserted itself.

"Well, Mr. Doherty," she said, "What do you have to say for yourself?"

"Crap," I thought. "How can she know?"

Soon enough, I found out that the linebacker was the store's security guard, and he had known my parents for years. They served together on a church committee. They had socialized enough that he knew or could guess who I was.

"Just wait 'til your father comes home," my mother said, the most terrible words in the English language. "You just wait, Mr. Doherty."

For the next two hours, I was made to stand in a corner of the dining room, without moving, waiting to hear the sounds of my dad coming home from work. And I got spanked until I howled.

I know now that spanking a child isn't the best way to parent, or at least that's what most educators and psychologists would have us believe. Yet all my friends were punished the same way. And none of them, as far as I know, ended up in prison.

Lancelot and Guinevere

In 1953, when I was 8, *Knights of the Round Table*, starring Robert Taylor as Lancelot and Ava Gardner as an unlikely Guinevere, ran for several weeks at the felicitously named Avalon Theater not far from Our Lady of Peace Church.

All the kids on our block went to see it at least once a week during its run. The crew included Ginny Duffy, my next-door neighbor, the Ross boys, who were distant cousins, Cyril Hughes, Pat Fagan, Jack Ford, and a fat girl whose name I must have repressed since she later kicked my ass in a fight.

For the boys, the attraction was the knights jousting. For the girls, it was the ladies of the court simpering over Lancelot, Galahad, Gawain, and Percival. Afterward, we galloped home along 79th Street imagining ourselves to be mounted on steeds, jousting with one another.

On weekday afternoons, between showings of the movie, with swords made out of broken broomsticks or branches snapped from the neighborhood's smaller trees and garbage can lid shields, we fought our way up and down the alleys, whacking away at each other manfully, the clanging of the lids filling the air.

On one of those afternoons, Ginny and I devised a game of our own. I was Lancelot and she was Guinevere. We built a castle for ourselves with a chenille bedspread hung over a clothesline in the backyard of the Duffys' apartment. The sun was high — but inside, the dappled shadows were soft and magical, making Ginny look like the princess she was playing.

Though we'd known each other all our lives and played together many times, I'd never thought of her as anything but a nuisance. But in our castle, with her green eyes and red hair and dimpled cheeks, I found her beautiful. I leaned toward her, garbage can lid in one hand and a crooked stick in the other, and kissed her. It was a long kiss, and I looked to see if her eyes were closed. They were. It was a perfect moment that I knew I wouldn't forget.

Perhaps she was as surprised as I was by the kiss. For when it was done, we both jumped backward, as if jolted by a shock, and looked around, hoping we hadn't been discovered. Then she smiled. I didn't know what to do, so I ran out of the tent, screaming a war cry and leaving my Guinevere standing there behind me.

Ginny Duffy and I never kissed again.

Ginny's father was a Chicago cop. Several years later, he was shot and badly wounded. According to a story that became famous in the neighborhood, when the police arrived on the scene, they found Mike crawling in the direction of the nearest hospital, saying the Act of Contrition at the top of his lungs, over and over again. His wife Peg, called by his fellow officers and told he was wounded and being treated at South Shore Hospital, took the time to squirm into a girdle, brush her hair, and put on full make-up as if, she said, she was going to mass. "What was I ever thinking?" she was reported to have said. "The man could have been dead before I ever got there."

After high school, Ginny joined a convent of cloistered nuns, sisters locked away from the world, forgoing speech and meat and most other pleasures. About 20 years after he was shot, her father died. Soon afterward, Ginny left the convent.

I'd like to think she remembered our childish kiss and decided the cloistered life was not for her.

Years later, after we had moved to Florida, I heard that Ginny had gotten heavy and strange, spending hours walking through the neighborhood talking to herself, shaking her head. Maybe she was praying. Maybe she was wishing she hadn't gone into the convent. I don't know. What I know is that Ginny occupied a large space in my memory, even though I couldn't really remember what she looked like.

Once, much later, drinking in a bar on the island of St. Thomas, I saw a red-haired woman who, for some reason, made me think of Ginny. I almost spoke to her before I realized she was much too young, young enough to be my daughter.

In Vino Veritas

The photograph is small, blurred, scarred by time. My mother snapped it using a Kodak box camera with a lens no bigger than a dime. I don't remember her taking the picture or me standing on the front stoop of the family's four-flat in a white suit, smiling. Though Father Murphy and the nuns had told me it was to be one of the defining moments of my life, I don't remember receiving Holy Communion that day. I recall neither the taste of the wafer nor any sudden welling up of wonder at Christ's body and blood transubstantiated into bread and wine.

I do remember the party that followed.

My uncles — Kevin, the redhead, his face lined from laughter and working in the sun, and Vincent, the politician, his eyes scouting the room for opportunities — stood in one corner drinking with my father. My Grandaunt Na, born Mary Hawkins but always called Na (it always made me think of a hare-lipped goat), was perched on the front of the sofa, a glass of Port in hand, looking for small children to frighten. Grandpa Mike, Mom's father, sat in the corner, folded in his dark, wool suit, mute as a tree.

The neighbors were there — the women helping my mother in the kitchen, the men smoking in the front room. And my brothers, Kevin and Patrick. And my cousins, trying and failing to behave and getting hushed and slapped every a few minutes.

I sat in the corner, in a wingback chair that was often my refuge at family gatherings in that room. But that day, I could not hide. I was the object of everyone's attention. Adults, one after another, came up to me, wishing me well and handing me envelopes containing holy cards and folded money.

Paper money was rare currency to children in those days, when a quarter would buy an afternoon at the Avalon Theater and an extra quarter would buy popcorn and candy and soda pop at the theater's counter with its five fountains, its huge Wurlitzer, and what was billed as the world's largest Oriental rug hanging from the ceiling.

I have a particular memory of Mike Molloy, whose card contained a five-dollar bill, a gift so large it made me tremble with thoughts of toys and candy and maybe a book from Marshall Field's. I still have that card. I remember, too, that Mary Flatley, my godmother, was there that day. She was a beautiful woman — beautiful almost beyond belief, I thought. I remember the sparkle in her eyes and the aroma of Chanel No. 5 as she bent forward to kiss me on the cheek.

Dinner was a fancy affair, with the good silver and the plates we used only on special occasions and crystal wine and water glasses. There was a standing rib roast and potatoes and vegetables and, for dessert, strawberry shortcake, made, as usual, not with cake but with over-baked biscuits. (I always ate only the strawberries and whipped cream.) There was a silver serving dish filled with olives, and candles in a candelabra as ornate as a cathedral, white candles that guttered all through the meal even though it was the middle of the day. There was laughter, too, and, of course, arguments about the Infallibility of the Pope and about Adlai and Ike and, as always, the Cubbies.

Before the feast, Uncle Kevin had gathered my brothers and me in a loose half circle and told us, once again, stories about his time as a flyer. But he never talked about the time his bomber crashed, killing the pilot and copilot. Afterward, the adults gathered in the front room and the children were let outside to play in the last light of the day.

I remember going back to the dining room to snack on the leftovers and noticing a half-bottle of wine, tawny Port, on the sideboard. I don't know what possessed me but I poured half a glass and drank it, gagging as it went down. Almost immediately, I felt the drink, mild as it was, hit my solar plexus like a fist, taking my breath away. I poured another half-glass of the cloying, bittersweet wine and drank it down.

The next thing I remember is wandering into the front room and climbing into my godmother's lap, smelling her perfumed hair and feeling the softness of her breasts. She kissed me. And I remember thinking that my life could never, ever get any better. My head was spinning but my senses were full. I did not know what they were full of at the time. Now I do.

When she kissed me in our makeshift "castle," Ginny Duffy had set the standard for my ideal girl — virtuous and virginal. And now Mary Flatley was my ideal woman — comforting and sexual.

Little did I know, then, that I was to spend the rest of my life searching for a reprise of those two perfect moments in my young life — not with Mary Flatley or Ginny Duffy and not very often with wine, but with women named and nameless and drink, always drink, that tamed me, unmanned me, beat me into the dirt, and eventually made me what I became, both good and bad.

Here's How

Sometime late in 1956, I was jerked from sleep by the sound of my mother sobbing. I sat up in my bunk bed and saw her standing just inside my bedroom door, face in her hands, shoulders heaving.

"Your grandfather is dead," she managed to gasp after a long moment. "My father is dead."

Old Mike Molloy was more a ghost to me than a real presence. A farmer's son, he had come to America as a young man. After getting a place to live and a job, he sent for Delia, his childhood sweetheart. She had been working as a servant in Ireland, but now joined him as his bride.

Mike had been a longshoreman like my father. And like my father, he eventually became the local longshoremen's union president.

By the time I was born, he'd retired. Delia was dead — I have no recollection of her at all — and he spent most of his time in his upstairs bedroom in the house he shared with my Uncle Kevin.

I remember him always with a book in his hand, either a well-worn Bible or his copy of *Speeches From the Dock*, a collection of speeches given by Irish patriots before they were executed by the Brits.

When he wasn't sitting in his rocking chair, creaking and reading, he paced in his room, thinking thoughts of County Mayo, imagining the long hilly walk from farm to town, and murmuring to Padraig Pearse and the other Fenians. Only rarely did he come down the stairs to greet us when we visited.

When he did, dressed in a white shirt buttoned to his throat, a pair of thick woolen trousers and a black cardigan sweater, winter or summer, his false teeth in the pocket of his sweater ready to be popped in his maw, old Mike would clench our shoulders in his strong hands and squeeze harder than he intended.

He'd comment on how tall we'd grown, even if it wasn't true. And then, when our parents weren't looking, he'd slip us coins, nickels and dimes and quarters, whispering a warning.

"Don't tell your ma or pa. This is our little secret," he'd say, his thick black eyebrows, flecked with dandruff, lowering conspiratorially.

Now he was dead, felled by a heart attack, and my mother was weeping. I had no idea what to say, none at all.

His wake was held a few days later at Sheehy's Funeral Home on Ashland Avenue, not far from the house he and Delia had shared. My recollection of the affair is dim. But I do remember that my brothers and I were dressed in black suits. And I remember not wanting to look at the body, but being forced not only to look but to kiss the wrinkled lips, lips hard and cool as concrete. I remember not feeling much of anything, certainly not thinking of my own mortality.

I remember my mother's tears, my dad holding her up, the two of them kneeling side by side with the three of us ranged to their left as the priest hurried through the rosary, all 15 decades.

What I remember most, though, is the fact that there was a bar right inside the funeral parlor, a place where the men gathered to drink while the women and the handful of teetotalers — there are never many at an Irish wake — stayed upstairs, mourning.

My uncle Kevin, still a young man but his face already worn by drink, his nose boasting a tracery of red veins just below the surface, took me to the bar.

"The boy's grandpa just died," he said to the barman. "How about a nice drink for the lad?"

"Sorry for your trouble," the barman said, words as old as Ireland herself. He slid two glasses in our direction and quickly poured from a bottle held in his right hand.

The glass was, I'd later learn, a rocks glass. Short and squat, stolid and serious, its cool shape filled my hand nicely, as if it had been designed just for me. The liquid it contained — there was no ice — glowed almost red in the light of the bar. My uncle picked up his glass, much fuller than mine, looked at me and smiled, more sad than happy.

"*Sláinte*," he said. "Here's how."

He raised his glass to his lips and tossed off the drink, his eyes widening slightly as the booze hit his throat.

I lifted my glass to my lips, took a breath and held it, then tilted my head back and drank it down. My eyes watered. And then I coughed, spitting out some of it. But enough went down. Almost instantly I experienced a replay of what I'd felt when I drank wine at my First Communion, only in spades.

I felt the liquor hot in my throat, then warm in my gut. I felt something as powerful as a fist to the base of my skull. Then I felt a switch click in my head. It felt like on to off. No, off to on. I was okay. Hell, I was better than okay. I licked my lips and grinned up at my uncle.

He laughed and ordered me another. That was plenty. I barely made it from the bar to a table in the corner where my dad sat with a few politicians and longshoremen who had come to pay their respects to old Mike Molloy. I sat with them, feeling warm and protected. Later, perhaps much later, I woke up with a headache and a fuzzy tongue. God, I loved it.

The Village Idiot

During my growing up years in Chicago, and indeed for years after that, girls and then women were as alien to me as creatures from another planet. They were all mysterious and frightening.

It did not help that I had no sisters and that the sexes were segregated at Our Lady of Peace. Even at recess, there was a line of demarcation painted across the middle of the big asphalt playground, with a clench-faced nun standing guard, her three-edged ruler at the ready.

I wondered what was under the blue skirts the girls wore, and I told myself I shouldn't care. But I did care. So, naturally, my friends and I tried to find out. When the playground guardian turned her back, we dashed into the forbidden female territory. With all the girls screaming, and knowing I had just seconds to achieve my objective, I'd single out a target and rush past her, reaching down and flipping up the bottom of her skirt, hoping to catch a glimpse of... I didn't know what, but something worth the effort, of that I was sure.

My parents, of course, never mentioned sex beyond a warning from my father that if I touched myself too much down there I'd go blind or mad or both. So I got my sex education where I could... mostly from Jack Farley, a large, rather head-heavy and slack-jawed, boy in my class.

Before the first bell rang one day, Jack came up to me and announced breathlessly that he had found some "dirty" pictures in his brother's dresser drawer and would share them with me because, well, just because.

Jack and I were not really friends, so I had no idea why, of all the boys in the class, he had chosen me to share his treasure. In all likelihood, I now know, he sensed my naïveté and figured I'd be easily impressed. Whatever his motivation, he was right in assuming I would want to see those pictures. I had a mission to discover the mysterious power that lay between a girl's thighs.

After school, Jack and I raced the half-mile or so to his house, walked as nonchalantly as possible through the kitchen where his mother was preparing the family's dinner, speaking pleasantries as required, then half-tripped up the carpeted stairs to his room.

"I have to get these back in my brother's dresser before he sees they're gone," he said as he dug under his mattress. "If he knows I've been foolin' with his stuff, he'll kill me."

The pictures were on the backs of playing cards, six of them taken from some deck that had probably been produced in Mexico. In each one, the same pudgy, bored-looking, dark-haired and dark-eyed *señora* or *señorita* sat or lay on what looked like a horse-hair sofa, over which hung a crucifix, as if to remind me I was sinning.

In every pose, she exposed herself — her heavy breasts and the furry gash between her legs — without a hint of passion or even involvement. She was unattractive, off-putting, and yet I couldn't stop staring, my mouth hanging open, as Jack moaned and rubbed himself through his corduroys.

"Wow," he said.

"Wow," I echoed.

I couldn't really link the woman in the pictures with any of the girls I knew at school and saw at church each Sunday morning. I surely couldn't link her to my mom. Not my mother! I almost said it aloud.

"So," I asked, my voice a croak, "what do you do? I mean how do you... you know?"

"Do it?" Jack asked.

"Yes."

Smirking, he launched into an explanation of the sex act, an explanation that involved anal sex and, after a gestation period of several weeks, the birth of a baby expelled from the woman's backside.

And I believed him.

Still, as ignorant about sex as I was, my life was not without romance. By the time I was 11, when my dad started talking about leaving his job and moving the family to Florida and we visited Clearwater on Florida's west coast looking for property, my friends started having what we called "boy-girl parties."

These were usually birthday parties, held in someone's "finished" basement, where a handful of kids would gather for chips, birthday cake, and some sort of warm punch served in cardboard cups with little flip-out handles that were too small for even the smallest of 11-year-old fingers.

A stack of 45s would be put on a record player not much bigger than a cigar box, and the boys and girls would stand on opposite sides of the room and listen, rocking back and forth, always out of sync with the music, seemingly an Irish trait.

I remember listening to the Rhythm Orchids' cut of "Party Doll," and all of us giggling when Buddy Knox sang, "I'll make love to you, to you."

At one of those parties, I screwed up my courage enough to ask a girl named Phyllis to dance with me. Until then, the only person I'd ever danced with was my mother, either at some wedding or in our living room as she tried to teach me how to step and glide in the box step, still the only dance I can do comfortably. Now, though, I took raven-haired Phyllis in my arms and moved slowly around the room, amazed by the feel and smell of her. She wasn't my godmother, didn't smell that sweet, had no breasts to speak of, but she certainly would do until something better came along.

At some point, she smiled down at me — the girls are always taller than the boys when you're 11 — and I knew I loved her.

Over the next few weeks and months, as we got ready to move south, where my father would build a motel and live the life of someone he called "Reilly," Phyllis and I danced at every opportunity. Once or twice, when some joker switched off the lights in the middle of a dance, we'd sway together clumsily and kiss faster than a blink. I even held her hand a few times. But that was as far as our love was destined to go.

I don't think I even said good-bye to her before the day of our move, when we loaded all our belongings into our two cars, the old Plymouth and a 1954 Chrysler Dad bought for Mom to drive, and headed down Highway 41.

Years later, after I was married for the second time, I said something to my parents about the lack of sex education in the Doherty household. "You know," I said, "I learned about sex from Jack Farley"

My father looked as if he didn't remember who Jack Farley was. My mother gasped, then laughed.

"Jack? Oh, the poor thing," she said, shaking her head as she stared down at her magazine. "He died before he got out of high school. You remember," she said to my father, who nodded just to keep himself out of the conversation.

"He only had an IQ of about 70," my mother said. "In the Old Country, he'd have been the village idiot. But you know," she added, "the Irish say the idiots are saints. They can't really sin. So I guess Jack is in heaven."

I kept my mouth shut.

THE EVOLUTION OF A WISE ASS

I Didn't Know Girls Farted

In my files, I have a newspaper clipping from the September 2, 1957, *Clearwater Sun*, the daily paper for the then-small town just north of St. Petersburg.

The picture shows my family in front of the motel my parents had just built on the as yet undeveloped south end of Clearwater Beach. My dad, a young man in the picture, sits on a lawn chair, my mother beside him in another chair. My brothers and I stand behind them, Pat to the left, me in the middle, and Kevin behind my father on the right.

I am, at age 12, skinny, with a flat-top haircut, as awkward and baffled by the world as some newborn animal. I'm wearing a short-sleeved polo shirt, striped. I remember how I hated that shirt.

The photo is accompanied by an article, maybe 450 words, with no byline. The headline...

Clearwater Motel Owner Formerly From Ireland

The first sentence of the story...

It's a long, long way to Tipperary.

It was a slow news day, I guess, but almost all days were slow in Clearwater in 1957, when the opening of a motel by a chap all the way from far-off Ireland was worthy of an article and photo in the paper.

According to the article, my parents got the idea to build a motel when, on a vacation in 1954, they stumbled across a vacant, man-made finger of land created by the dredging of the roughly two-mile-wide bay that lay between Clearwater Beach and the mainland. I have no recollection of that vacation, though I was almost certainly in the car, sweating in the back seat along with my brothers, when my parents "stumbled across" the property.

I do remember how earnestly my parents had dreamed of the day when the family would be able to escape the cold and grime and hard work of Chicago to live a better life in Florida. Not long after my grandfather's death, we made the move.

While the motel — it was called the Sea Cloud — was being built, we lived in an old frame house not far from the Gulf of Mexico, about two miles from the motel site.

The house was a bungalow, gray or pale green, with a screened porch. It lay sprawled across about a half-acre of land surrounded by scrub palms and Australian pines that left the ground covered with dried palm fronds and brown pine needles and cones.

I drove by there not long ago. The house, and those that were around it, are long gone, replaced by a five-story condominium, one of hundreds of buildings that now glut the island I remember so fondly.

Looking at the spot where the house once stood, I remembered the smell of the place at low tide, a bitter mix of saltwater and sea bottom, with a touch of mildew.

After a few weeks, my dad went back to Chicago to wrap up the sale of the apartment building and his complicated dealings with the union. I don't know the details, but the break-up was not amicable. I figure some of the hard men he'd spent time with in the bellies of the ships and the grain elevators and the union hall were simply angry that one of their own was leaving, breaking free. In any event, we boys were left in Florida with Mom, who was kept busy overseeing the construction of the motel.

Almost as soon as we unpacked, we were enrolled in new schools. Kevin was enrolled as a freshman in a Catholic high school and Pat was put in the fifth grade at the public grammar school in Clearwater. I was enrolled in the town's junior high school, an old complex of buildings rumored to have been a Confederate hospital in the Civil War. The school, brick with tall, narrow windows, dark hallways, and sudden and unexpected turnings and dead ends, could easily have done duty as a prison. I hated it.

For the first time in my life, I was taught by someone not dressed to look like a penguin. I had to take a bus to school instead of walking with my kid brother. I had to buy something called "lunch tickets" and eat in a cafeteria instead of walking two blocks home to have a sandwich with my mother or, as I sometimes did, eat with friends in the schoolyard. I had to go to class with kids I didn't know — not just boys but girls, and I had not been in a classroom with a girl since the third grade.

I was terrified. I knew I wouldn't fit in and the knowledge made me want to puke.

My time in public school — I was there about 18 months, all told — was every bit as bad as I expected it to be. In English class, the very first day, the teacher told us to write a sonnet. He was a strange little man, only about five feet tall, with a Hitleresque mustache. And he addressed us as *mesdames et messieurs*. Though it was about 90 degrees in the room (no air conditioning), hot enough to bring beads of sweat to the brows of even the picture-perfect southern belles in the class, he wore a wool jacket with leather patches, a starched but wilted white shirt, and a bow tie that hung limply beneath his collar.

I thought he was insufferable. (And he was.) At the end of that first class, I had to force myself to go up to this little man and tell him I couldn't write a sonnet because, God help me, I had no more idea what a sonnet was than how to fly around the room.

Math class wasn't much better. While the other students were plugging away at word problems ("After her party, Suzie had 6 1/3 boxes of cookies left over. She gave each of her 4 guests the same amount of the leftover cookies to take home. How many boxes of cookies did she give each guest?"), I felt trapped in a pit of quicksand, sinking fast.

There was also a class in some subject I'd never heard of, something called Civics, and a class in woodshop. What the hell was that about? Class after class proved to me, beyond a doubt, that the parochial school system in Chicago was designed to produce dolts and that the sainted nuns at Our Lady of Peace had no idea how to prepare students for the real world down in Florida.

Then there was the business with girls. I was no more prepared to deal with the girls in this school than I was prepared to divvy up cookies among my party guests. When I stood any closer to a girl than six feet or so, I started sweating, my tongue swelled to fill my mouth, and I began breathing rapidly through my nose, remembering, as I did, the pictures Jack Farley had shown me.

When other boys and girls chatted together, making plans to go to a football game or one of the dances that were regularly hosted by the city as a way to keep Clearwater's youth from running amok, I stood off to one side, unable to look anybody, boy or girl, in the eye.

After several weeks, I suddenly noticed that the girl who sat in front of me in homeroom (another novelty) was always turning around to give me a big smile, a smile that put dimples in her cheeks. She had blue eyes. She was tall and slender, a little taller than I was and a little skinnier. She had no breasts, but who cared? What she did have was long blonde hair and she was a girl, by God, a living, breathing girl. A cute one, so cute that she made me want to rip my heart out and hand it to her.

I fell in love. We hadn't really spoken up to that point, but it didn't matter. I imagined how she'd look in a long, white wedding dress. I could almost see the little house we'd occupy not far from Ozzie and Harriet and David and Ricky. I could almost taste the little woman's pot roast. I wondered how it would feel when we finally did "it" — the strange "it" that had been described by Jack Farley.

I screwed up my courage and asked her if she'd go to a dance with me. My parents would drive, of course. She said yes and I felt like I was swimming through the air. For a couple of days, I was happier than I'd ever been in my life, looking forward to our "date." Then one morning, it may have been the morning of the dance, something terrible happened.

She was wearing a red and blue skirt with a pure white blouse, adorable as a kitten. I sat at my desk, right behind her, wondering what it would be like when we were finally together. And she farted. Loudly.

I was devastated. I had no idea that girls ever burped or picked their noses or scratched their behinds or did any of the things that I, and all my friends, routinely did either for pleasure or simply to occupy time when there was nothing better to do.

Alas, I was from a culture that puts women on pedestals... the Blessed Virgin... our own sainted mothers. If you want to get in a fight with an Irish kid, say something about his mother. It doesn't even have to be particularly nasty. The "M" word will barely be out of your mouth before the first punch will be thrown.

But that's beside the point. Because back then, on that day, there was a girl, the girl I was going to take to a dance, the girl I was going to marry and do "it" with — and she farted. My heart was broken because I knew I could never think of her the same way again. So after homeroom, I caught up with her in the hall. Surrounded by babbling, swarming teenagers, I broke our date.

Later, I discovered that she was the daughter of an automobile dealer, one of the richest men in town. Having, by that time, learned some of the things girls and women were capable of, things that put farting in perspective, I knew I should have overlooked the fart and taken her to the dance.

As if my first experience with female farting weren't disheartening enough, I also had to contend with gym class and naked boys.

When I enrolled at Clearwater Junior High, I was issued a bunch of used textbooks, a locker assignment, and instructions to buy a pair of red shorts and a white T-shirt with a red CJHS logo on it. I was also told to buy something called a "jockstrap."

"What for?" I asked.

For Phys Ed, I was told.

Phys Ed.

Even today, the words fill me with revulsion. As a skinny, uncoordinated 12-year-old, I was terrified. We're all, of course, frightened by the unknown. And I knew nothing at all about Phys Ed. In Catholic school, Physical Education was pretty much limited to running around in the schoolyard — or, if you were a girl, jumping rope or playing jacks. The nuns didn't have time to waste on anything like structured exercise. They were too busy making sure the boys and girls didn't stray from their own territory in the schoolyard, as well-defined as the DMZ in Korea.

Until then, I'd never played an organized game of baseball, never lined up with teammates in a football game, never really done much of anything in terms of sports.

But that wasn't the worst of it. I'd also never changed in a locker room or showered with boys other than my brothers. "Oh, God," I thought. "Why me? Why couldn't we have just stayed up in Chicago where I could go to Catholic school and keep my clothes on? So what if I didn't know what a sonnet was or how to do word problems, at least I wouldn't have to get naked in front of strangers."

The reality turned out to be even worse than my worst fears. Walking into the locker room for the first time, I found myself in an alien landscape of exposed pipes, dirty tile, an open shower room with about a dozen shower heads, and a horde of boys who — it seemed to me — loved nothing more than running around naked, flicking towels at each other's asses, and laughing at jokes I really did not understand.

What was intolerable was that I found it impossible to strip in such a way that I was completely unobserved. No matter which way I stood in front of my locker, no matter how I twisted or turned, hopped from one foot to the other, ducked my head, no matter what I did, I could see someone staring at me, ready to jeer or at least point.

Somehow, I managed to change into my CJHS T-shirt, rapidly pull down my pants, and just as quickly pull up the shorts. Forget the jockstrap. As far as I was I concerned, I didn't need it. It looked to me like nothing more than an obscene version of the sling David used to slay Goliath. I had no idea how to wear it, and was not about to ask. Burning with embarrassment, I sidled out of the locker room and followed a group of boys to one of the school's several playing fields.

My only desire was to fade from view like the Cheshire Cat in *Alice in Wonderland*. Instead, I was almost immediately chosen to play on one side in a game of slow-pitch softball. The boy who chose me, I'm sure, thought it was a great joke at the expense of the new kid. The game is forgettable — except for the remarkable fact that, in the third inning, I got a hit.

The pitcher, a bully I would come to hate and avoid, threw two fastballs over the heart of the plate, pitches I swung at and missed. Then, smirking, he threw the ball right at my head as hard as he could.

Instinctively, I yelped, jumped back, and wielded the bat as a defensive weapon. Somehow, the bat and ball collided and the ball went skittering in the direction of the pitcher's mound. I guess everybody was so surprised that I was still alive that no one bothered to try to catch the ball until I was standing — breathless, but safe — on first.

After that, I was never again chosen to play sides in any game. Having terrified me, the other kids were eager to forget me. Eventually, I threw the shorts and jockstrap away, showed up for Phys Ed in a pair of jeans, told the teacher I'd lost the shorts and couldn't afford to buy another pair and was, blessedly, left alone.

My Phys Ed grades in junior high never got above D, but I didn't mind. It was worth it to avoid the public shower.

The Queer and the Coward

Jan and I could have been friends. We were much alike. Though he was dark with dark hair, and I am fair with red hair, we were almost brothers in terms of our discomfort in crowds, our inability to look people in the eye, our physical ineptitude, and, let's face it, our weakness.

Jan and I had no classes together. We'd pass in the hall as we moved from one room to another in that old, two-story school building. He was the only one I ever saw in that school who carried a slide rule in his shirt pocket.

Since he was different, he was fair game for the bullies — and, of course, so was the new, skinny, glasses-wearing boy from Chicago. What happened was almost choreographed.

One day, during lunch break, I was sitting outside under a large, moss-hung oak, when a bully — the same one who tried to hit me with the pitched ball — appeared from nowhere, followed by three or four of his friends. Each wore the uniform of the rebel, a white T-shirt with the sleeves rolled up, jeans, and motorcycle boots, though it would be several years before any of them could get a driver's license.

He stood in front of me, arms akimbo, glaring down.

"Did you hear what that queer Jan said about you?" he asked.

Though I had only a dim understanding of what it meant to be queer, I knew it wasn't good. I knew, too, from the bully's tone of voice, that I was in some kind of trouble.

"Yeah," one of his cohorts said. "He said you were afraid of him."

"I said no way," another of the bully's followers said. "I said nobody's afraid of you, you queer."

"What are you gonna do about it?" the bully challenged me. "You're not gonna take it, are you?"

I looked up at them. Their eyes had a kind of glassy look, the way a dog's eyes look when he's panting over a bone that's just out of reach.

I'm sure that, at some level, I knew they were setting me up, making me an actor in a play they'd written for their own amusement. How much fun would it be to force a boy named Kieran to fight a boy named Jan?

"C'mon," one of them said. "You can't let that queer get away with it."

I mumbled something about not caring one way or the other. Jesus, just leave me alone, I thought. "I don't have a problem with him," I squeaked.

The bully and his friends were not about to accept that as an answer. They began taunting me. They said I was as queer as Jan and a sissy. Then they called me a chicken. A *chicken*. That, I could not tolerate.

I got to my feet and walked over to where Jan was sitting. He saw us coming and put his sandwich down, rewrapping it carefully in wax paper before putting it back into its brown paper bag.

"I hear you said I was afraid of you," I said.

Jan shook his head. "No," he said. "No I didn't."

The bully and his friends danced around us. "Fight! Fight! Fight!" they chanted.

"C'mon, Doherty," the bully said. "You can take this faggot." He patted me on the shoulder. And though I knew it was wrong, though I knew what I was doing was as wrong as it could be, it felt so good when the bully I couldn't stand patted my shoulder that I clenched my fists and raised them the way my uncle Kevin had shown me long ago in my grandfather's kitchen.

Jan didn't move. He just sat there with his hands folded as if he were praying. A circle of kids formed around us, yelling and clapping. Jan looked up at me and shook his head as if to say that we didn't have to do this.

"Punch him!" somebody shouted.

I did. I punched his shoulder. Jan didn't move.

"Hit him!" somebody else screamed.

I reached out and slapped his face.

Slowly, Jan got to his feet. He took the slide rule out of his pocket and put it on the table next to his lunch bag. That's what I remember most clearly. The deliberate way he took the slide rule from his pocket and put it on the table. I noticed, too, that his hand was as steady as if he were reaching out to switch on a light. Then he turned to me. I didn't give him a chance even to make a fist. I punched him, hit him flush on his left cheek.

"Fight! Fight!" everyone shouted.

It sounded like there were hundreds of them. And it felt good. I swung with my right hand and grunted when my fist met Jan's nose. Blood spurted and he held his hand to his face to try to keep it from running down the front of his shirt. Immediately, I wanted to reach out and help him, maybe even take him in my arms to comfort him. But I didn't because I couldn't.

Instead, I had to stand there grinning, though I felt like I was going to puke.

"Had enough?" I shouted. "Had enough, queer?"

God, how I hoped he'd just walk away. I breathed easy when I saw him shake his head and turn to his lunch bag and slide rule, his shirt all bloody.

As fast as the crowd had gathered, it dissipated. In seconds, we were alone. Not even the bully and his friends stuck around once the "fight" was over. There was only me and Jan.

I wanted to say I was sorry. I wanted to say I had to do what I had to do if I wanted to fit in. Surely, he'd understand if anybody would. I looked down at my right hand. My knuckles were bleeding, cut by his teeth. I remembered my mom telling me that the human mouth is filthy, filled with germs. I stared at my hand, hoping I wouldn't get an infection.

Jan gathered his belongings and walked away.

So there it was. The same desire to fit in, the need for approval that made me hate Sammy Ross for making fun of me had now seduced me to the point where I'd hurt someone else, hurt him physically, shamed him, just to gain the favor of boys I'd probably never see again, boys I didn't even care about.

I'd like to think that if I had it to do over, I'd have the courage to stand up to the bully and his friends. I'd like to think that Jan and I could have talked and maybe become friends. I'd like to think a lot of things could have been different.

But I don't know. I know myself well enough to suspect I would have made the same cowardly choice. That doesn't make me proud or happy. But that's the way it is.

Holy Knockers

Not long after we moved to Florida, my father took me with him to a retreat, three days of contemplation and prayer at the Trappist Monastery of the Holy Spirit in the red-dirt hill country not far from Atlanta, Georgia.

We drove up Highway 19 out of Clearwater and stopped at a diner for lunch. Walking into the restaurant at my dad's side, I felt like, man, I wished the moment would never end. Me and my old man, traveling together.

At the end of the day, we wheeled off the highway and turned in to the monastery.

I expected a massive stone building, with a bell tower like the European monasteries I'd seen in pictures. Instead, it was a collection of not very impressive wooden buildings at the end of a bumpy road. There was a barn that had been converted into a church, hastily constructed living quarters for the monks, and a refashioned farmhouse where visitors were housed.

We were greeted by a Trappist priest, a monk in white and black robes. (The brothers, who were not ordained, wore plain brown robes.) The priest, who was stout and kind of soft looking, didn't talk much. He smiled and nodded and then smiled some more as he showed us up a flight of stairs and down a narrow corridor to our rooms.

I spent most of our three-day stay in the church, a narrow, pine board building not much larger than a typical one-bedroom home. The church was the heart of the monastery. It was there that the monks, when they weren't working like dogs in the fields or illustrating manuscripts or building what would ultimately become a huge, Gothic, concrete cathedral, chanted their hours throughout the day, beginning with Lauds at 2:00 a.m. and ending with Compline, the most stirring of the chanted hours, at 7:00 p.m. The dark wooden church, with its round stained glass window of the Blessed Virgin high over a plain altar and its unadorned wooden seats along both walls, the beautiful rhythm of the Gregorian chant, antiphon and response, basically unchanged in a millennium, attracted me, calmed me, suffused me with what I thought was a divine calling.

I found a copy of the Divine Office of St. Benedict in the back of the church, where outsiders could kneel during services, and sneaked it into my room and into my suitcase. I did not recognize the irony of stealing a prayer book and certainly don't remember feeling guilty.

An unrepentant thief, I left the monastery and headed back to Florida, convinced I had been chosen to lead the Trappist way of life, a life of silence and prayer and labor, *laborare est orare*, lived according to the Rule of Benedict. I was so sure that for a time I tried to read my stolen prayer book every day and avoid sin. I even announced my intention to my family.

Almost every Irish Catholic boy has thoughts of the priesthood, and many Irish Catholic families in the 1950s and 60s had one son who was a man of the cloth and another who wore a badge and blue serge. But my parents knew me much better than I knew myself. While they threw no roadblocks in my path, they didn't go out of their way to encourage me. They knew, as I didn't, that my romance with the monastery was but a short-term fling, one I'd enjoy only so long as there were no consequences.

Vaguely suspecting that I was teasing God (and kidding myself) with the idea of becoming a priest, I tried to mitigate what I feared would be a heavy price for my hypocrisy. For a few weeks, I went to mass more willingly, I prayed before I went to sleep, and I stopped stealing money from Mom's purse and Dad's pants.

Even those half-hearted attempts stopped soon after the eighth grade started, my personal vision of holiness eclipsed by a pair of what my peers and I called titties or knockers.

I was sitting in the junior high school library, probably goofing off, when a girl entered wearing the uniform of the day: a short-sleeved cashmere sweater with a circle pin, an honest-to-God poodle skirt, and white socks and penny loafers. She was heartbreakingly lovely, a petite version of Mary Tyler Moore on "The Dick Van Dyke Show" — except for one, or rather two, things.

Her breasts were huge, the biggest breasts I'd ever seen. Hell, I thought, with my limited experience, breasts couldn't get any bigger or more perky. They were awesomely attention grabbing. Somehow I managed to stutter an inane greeting and introduce myself. Her name was Patricia. Patti. Patti Dornbos. She was in the seventh grade. And from that day forward, I had no intention whatsoever of becoming a Trappist or any other kind of cleric.

We became — on and off, but mostly off — a couple. We would date, for a time, the way all 13-year-olds dated, sneaking kisses in the movies, holding hands on the beach, trading notes, and generally acting foolish. Then, for a time, we wouldn't date.

I had other girlfriends when I was in high school: Janice, who broke my heart when I was 16, and Gretchen, who broke it a year or so later, and a skinny girl named Sunny Bobo, who water-skied and fished for snapper and made me laugh like hell, and a red-haired girl so tall I had to stand on my tiptoes to kiss good night. But Patti was there for years and years, always a friend and often more than that.

Though meeting Patti put an end to any possibility that I would become a Trappist, I had already committed to spending three weeks of the summer between eighth grade and high school working at the monastery as a "family brother." This was the title given to young men who were seriously — or in my case, not seriously — considering the monastic life.

This time, I made the trip on my own, the first time I was on an airplane. When the plane landed in Atlanta, I was met by a white-and-black-robed priest who didn't say a word as he led me to a pickup truck and drove to the monastery.

As a monk wannabe, I lived pretty much as a half-monk. I slept in a room in the guesthouse, worked with the brothers doing manual labor around the monastery farm, and joined the community in prayer in the church. I ate with the men on retreat, but was instructed to remain as silent as possible.

I still loved the chanting and the incense and the peacefulness, but I spent most of my time, in church or at work, thinking about Patti and her breasts. I hadn't yet worked up the courage to touch even one of them, let alone both, through her clothes. But I could imagine.

I worked a day or two with an elderly artisan, making stained glass windows. I shoveled silage from the back of a truck to a herd of milling cows and learned how to eat sorghum from the bottom of the silo, sorghum wet with fermented juices with enough kick to make a 13-year-old dizzy and happy. I carried ears of corn to pig pens and fed the pigs. And all the time I worked, I fantasized about Patti's knockers.

In my mind's eye, they were perfect, as if fashioned by Michelangelo. The question was, given the opportunity, what should I do with them? Should I approach them as if they were dangerous? Should I stroke them the way I'd stroke a puppy's head? Should I be aggressive and show them who's boss? I had no idea.

The fantasies continued, often accompanied by masturbating (a pastime I'd discovered by accident some time earlier). And I knew that for me — not for all men, but for me — true happiness was to be found not behind a monastery wall but, rather, in breasts.

I may not have had a divine calling, but I was enough of a Catholic to figure that by committing "self-abuse" on Holy Ground I was in for it, if not in this world, then certainly in the next. So along with the weight of constantly thinking about Patti's tits, I now had to carry a burden of guilt thinking about the boy — a priest swore this story was real — the boy who defiled himself on a Saturday night and then tried to take Communion on Sunday morning. As soon as the host touched his tongue, the priest said, blood began gushing from the boy's still open mouth.

He was dead before he hit the marble floor in front of the altar.

In the midst of my three-week stint at the monastery, I met a couple of local boys, teenagers, who worked for the brothers part-time. They told me they were going to Atlanta for some "fun," and invited me along for the ride.

I had to sneak out of the monastery. My holy hosts, I knew, would have looked askance at a 13-year-old going out for a night on the town.

When we got to Atlanta, we searched one of the city's seedier neighborhoods until we found a guy willing to buy us some beer in exchange for a couple of bucks. I remember drinking two or maybe three cans of beer in an alley somewhere near the downtown. The beer made me drunk as a coot, dizzy and ill, and even managed to drive thoughts of Patti's tits from my mind.

Later in my life, booze managed to erase any thoughts of those I supposedly loved. But back then, the only thing I was conscious of was that, once again, I felt the way I had when I drank at my First Communion and at my grandfather's wake. And I loved it. By the end of that night, I knew that what I wanted to do was to drink whatever I could, every time I had an opportunity.

And so I did.

Penance Hall

As a 13-year-old freshman in 1958, I was not prepared for the rigors of Jesuit high school. The Jesuit priests prided themselves on their education and insisted that their students meet their high standards.

My older brother, Kevin, had preceded me. A member of the chess club, swim team, and a starting guard on the football team, he had earned a reputation as an all-around good student with middling grades.

If the Jesuit fathers and the "misters" who were at the school for a required two-year teaching stint before their ordination expected a smaller, younger version of Kevin to grace their classrooms, they were to be surprised.

I was a lazy boy who never opened a textbook unless it was absolutely necessary. I cut classes and forged my mother's signature on excuses. If my academic potential was limited, my sports potential was even worse. Almost six feet tall, I was skinny, awkward, and had no interest in improving myself.

But that didn't deter the Jesuits. As one said when he sized me up on the first day, "You're a lump of coal, but give us some time. We'll turn you into a diamond."

For four years, we sparred, the Jesuits coming from one corner and me from the other. They fought their hearts out to make a man of me, but I did everything I could to defend myself against their efforts. I was forever going as far over the line as I could without getting expelled.

I was, as my father used to say, a punk — a boy who lacked courage and discipline, which meant I lacked character. I see now that I wanted attention, but I found it easier to get by being a wise ass than by buckling down and accomplishing something.

My *punkiness* extended to the area of faith. Although just weeks earlier I was considering a vocation in the priesthood, I quickly became a lapsed Catholic. I did not go to mass. I did not go to Confession. And I did not take Communion unless I had to.

Fifty years and a lake of booze turns the memory into a movie film with more charred spots than healthy celluloid. Still, I remember a lot about those years — most of it centering on Father Charles Lashley.

As the school's disciplinarian, it was one of his jobs to patrol the school searching for boys who were in violation of the rules. For underclassmen, those rules included not smoking on campus, not walking on the grass, not littering, and, of course, a host of stringent restrictions that kept order in the classrooms. He also saw to it that the students dressed properly — most wore ties — and kept their hair trimmed.

Father Lashley was an institution at the school. At least three generations of students left with stories about his prowess at spotting offenders. Raising his eyes to glare at the miscreant, he would point his index finger and say, "See me, boy!"

That's all. Three words. See. Me. Boy.

That meant: "Show up in my classroom at the end of the school day."

Not for nothing was the room called "Penance Hall." Father Lashley had the ability to dream up the strangest punishments. And the punishment needed to be completed before you were dismissed.

Usually, he could be seen walking slowly along one of the halls in his black cassock and white clerical collar, his right thumb hooked in the black sash he wore low on his hips the way a gunslinger wore a pistol belt. In his left hand, he carried his breviary, open to the prayer for the day. As he walked, it appeared that he never lifted his eyes from the page as his lips moved silently. However, it was impossible to break any rule without being noticed.

One day when I was walking down the hall, admittedly in need of a haircut, I saw Father Lashley approaching. I knew, just knew, I was in trouble. As I neared him, he nodded in my direction and said, "A moment, Doherty."

I stopped. And with one swift motion, he pulled out a pair of scissors he had tucked somewhere on his person and clutched a hunk of my hair.

"You need a trim," he said.

With that, he snipped off the hair so close to the skull that I had no choice but to get a buzz cut. Not my favorite hairstyle at the time.

Nabbed for jumping over one of the flowering hedges on the campus, I was sentenced to crafting 100 paper flowers out of tissue paper.

Then there were the cigarettes. In my junior year, I was caught smoking on campus. I was hiding behind a tree, puffing away on a Kool, when Lashley suddenly appeared from behind the tree next to mine and pointed his finger at me.

"Aha!" he cried. "See me, boy."

My punishment was to draw 1,000 packs of Kool cigarettes complete with a little picture on the front of each pack showing Willy the Penguin — Kool's mascot —puffing on a cigarette. Beneath each pack I had to print, *Willy the Penguin says it's not cool to smoke in school.*

I was in Penance Hall for the balance of my junior year and several weeks into the summer. That punishment ranked for years (may still, in fact) as the longest stint in Penance Hall by any student in the history of the school. Not much of a record, I'm afraid, but the only one I left behind.

Flunking the Test

From the very beginning, I did not drink the way anybody I knew drank. There were certainly plenty of clues, if I wanted to see them. And then there was the test…

Maybe you've seen the test. Maybe you even answered all 26 of the questions. Or perhaps you answered only a few of them and, knowing which way things were going, you stopped.

Every alcoholic I've ever met took this self-test at some point in his drinking career. It was developed by the National Council on Alcoholism to be used to determine whether an individual was an alcoholic or had the potential to become an alcoholic.

With thanks to the NCOA, here it is…

To determine whether alcohol is a problem for you, answer YES or NO to this series of questions.

1. Do you occasionally drink heavily after a disappointment, quarrel, or rough day?

YES

NO

2. When under pressure, do you always drink more heavily than usual?

YES

NO

3. Can you handle more liquor now than when you first started drinking?

YES

NO

4. On the " morning after," have you been unable to remember part of the evening before — even though friends say you didn't pass out?

YES

NO

5. When drinking with others, do you try to have a few extra drinks when they won't know it?

YES

NO

6. Are there certain occasions when you feel uncomfortable if alcohol is not available?

YES

NO

7. When you start drinking, are you in more of a hurry to get the first drink than you used to be?

YES

NO

8. Do you sometimes feel a little guilty about your drinking?

YES

NO

9. Are you secretly irritated when friends or family discuss your drinking?

YES

NO

10. Have you experienced memory blackouts more frequently?

YES

NO

11. Do you often want to drink more after friends have had enough?

YES

NO

12. Do you usually have a reason for occasions when you drink heavily?

YES

NO

13. When sober, do you often regret things you've done or said while drinking?

YES

NO

14. Have you tried to control your drinking by switching brands or following different plans?

YES

NO

15. Have you often failed to keep promises about controlling your drinking?

YES

NO

16. Have you tried to control your drinking by changing jobs or moving?

YES

NO

17. Do you try to avoid family or friends while drinking?

YES

NO

18. Are you having an increasing number of financial and work problems?

YES

NO

19. Do more people seem to be treating you unfairly without reason?

YES

NO

20. Do you eat very little or irregularly when drinking?

YES

NO

21. Do you sometimes have the morning "shakes" and relieve them with a drink?

YES

NO

22. Are you unable to drink as much as you once did?

YES

NO

23. Do you sometimes stay drunk for several days at a time?

YES

NO

24. Do you sometimes feel very depressed and wonder whether life is worth living?

YES

NO

25. After drinking, do you ever see or hear things that aren't there?

YES

NO

26. Do you get terribly frightened after drinking heavily?

YES

NO

According to the experts, if you answered "Yes" to just one of these questions, you are exhibiting symptoms of alcoholism.

If you answered "Yes" to three or more of the first eight questions, you are in the early stage of alcoholism.

If you answered "Yes" to three or more of the questions numbered from 9 to 21, you're in the middle stage of alcoholism.

If you said "Yes" to three or more of the last six questions, you are in the beginning of the final stage.

I don't remember the first time I took the test. That in itself is a pretty good sign I was drunk when I did it. I do remember taking the test when I was in my mid-20s. I had to take comfort in the fact that I didn't answer "Yes" to all the questions. I only answered "Yes" to 21 of the 26.

There are a couple of real problems with this test. It doesn't tell you how long your final stage might be and it doesn't tell you how bad things can get.

But I can.

When I speak now in front of other sober drunks, I joke that for low-bottom drunks like me, there should be a special test — a test with questions like these:

Did you ever run over yourself with your own car?

Did you ever get a sunburn on the roof of your mouth?

Did you ever pick up someone in a bar, hoping to score, and bring him/her home to meet your spouse or partner?

Did you ever urinate on the floor because you didn't want to give up your barstool?

I would have had to answer "Yes" to all those questions. And others having to do with lines I never thought I'd cross.

When I tell my story, I can see a few people, men and women both, who nod before they laugh. And I know they know. But even without the nods, we — those of us who were low-bottom drunks but have come back — can usually pick each other out in crowds, at meetings of sober alkys, or just walking down the street.

There's a wariness of the new, a skittishness with the present, a tendency to get "lost" for a few seconds while talking. There's also the proclivity to look at the world and see nothing except the past. And there is the humor — the crude, almost euphoric, humor that comes from having stood at the edge of the abyss. It's a gratitude that defies belief.

You'll usually find us sitting together at AA fellowship meetings just because we understand each other better than others, even other alcoholics, can. And make no mistake, there are alcoholics who didn't have to slide quite as far down as we did. It's not a matter of pride to be a low-bottom drunk. But it is a reality.

As I said, from the very beginning, I didn't drink the way anybody else I knew drank.

By the time I was in high school, I was drinking on weekends. If I had the money, a friend and I would drive to what we called "Colored Town" and search for someone leaning against a wall or stumbling down the street or drinking from a paper sack. It was easy to find a guy who would want to earn a couple of dollars for getting us a fifth of cheap vodka and two quarts of orange juice.

Then Jerry — that was my friend's name — and I would drive to some secluded spot where we'd each pour out half a bottle of orange juice and dump in half of the fifth. Then we'd drink it down, as fast as possible.

Jerry tried to keep up with me, but more than once he threw up before he finished his "cocktail." A time or two, I caught him surreptitiously dumping part of it when he figured I wasn't looking.

Not me. I was proud of the fact that at age 15 or maybe 16, I could drink a quart of screwdrivers, half vodka and half orange juice, without taking the bottle from my lips. And after I drank, I was comfortable. I'd even feel capable of going to one of the teen dances that were held almost every weekend. I could ask a girl to dance. I could dance. I could talk. I was able to laugh and equally able to fight. I was part of the world. Hell, I was on top of the world.

I didn't get drunk every weekend. Not because I didn't want to but because it simply was not possible. However, I did drink as often as I could and I got drunk every time I drank. That, after all, was the only reason to drink back then. It wasn't until later, when I was trying to come up with reasons not to quit, that I began talking about alcohol as a social lubricant, as a relaxant at the end of a tough day, as somehow my due because I worked so hard.

In the beginning, I was more honest. I drank to get… well, fucked up. And if I didn't get fucked up, my drinking wasn't successful.

My parents seemed not to know. They were busy running the small Clearwater Beach motel. Most of the time, I shared one of the empty motel rooms with my older brother or slept in a small addition to the owner's apartment, barely big enough to hold a bed. My parents trusted me, I guess. Or maybe they were just so absorbed with making a living that they didn't pay attention. In any case, they never looked askance, never said anything. At least not then.

Three Fingers of Rye

When I was 15, my mother and I went to New Orleans to visit my brother Kevin. He was studying at Loyola, preparing to be a dentist. I helped her drive the long miles up the gut of Florida, then along the Gulf through Mobile and Biloxi and Pass Christian until we crossed the Mississippi and landed in the French Quarter.

I immediately fell in love with the city. It was as if the whole thing had been designed specifically for me — the Garden District, the warehouse area (which was not gentrified then), Magazine Avenue, the old zoo. But most of all, I loved the French Quarter, with its funky eateries and smoke shops and junk stores and bars that stayed open around the clock.

I spent as much time as I could on Bourbon Street, taking in the gaudy lights, the drunken men, the hookers and transvestites lurking in doorways. I inhaled the aromas — the smell of garlic and fresh bread wafting out of the restaurants… the odor of stale beer emanating from the bars in the morning and combining with the lush fragrance of chicory coffee and beignets. And I listened to the music — the Dixieland jazz from the clubs… the bump and grind music from the stripper joints… the old, black men reluctantly playing "When the Saints Go Marching In" over and over again for the tourists at Preservation Hall.

Our first morning, Mom and I rode the trolley along Canal Street, ate Oysters Benedict for breakfast at Brennan's, visited the antique shops on Rue Royale, had pastel portraits done by a street artist, and said a quick prayer at St. Louis Cathedral.

My mother, thinking I wanted to be an artist, bought me a beret I never wore and an ascot I didn't appreciate. She also bought me an antique bloodstone ring that I eventually gave to a Mexican border-town whore whose name I can't remember.

We stayed in a guesthouse, one of the stately old homes that still line St. Charles Avenue. That first night, as my mother got ready for bed, I dressed in my spiffy new three-piece suit, tied a tie barely wider than a shoelace round my neck, and, with her permission, went "sightseeing" in the Quarter.

I started at a small, smoke-filled place, probably a workingman's dive. I sidled up to the bar manfully, between two rough-looking characters. I tried to look rough myself, not an easy task when you're too young to shave and only a couple of years out of Roy Rogers underpants. The fellow to my right ordered three fingers of rye — Old Overholt, a name I found fascinating and easy to remember. I ordered the same thing and almost gagged but tossed it down.

From there, I went to Pat O'Brien's. I took a seat and started drinking Hurricanes, the drink they're known for, concocted of rum and passion fruit juice and served in a glass that looks like a hurricane lamp. At one point, what I took to be a young woman wearing a party dress asked if she could join me. I, of course, said yes — and thought I had gotten lucky... until "she" took my hand and placed it on the erect cock under her dress. I yelped. She ran away.

That was the last thing I remember about that night.

When I awoke, furry tongued and headachy, I found my three-piece suit carefully arranged on a hanger, dangling from a tree limb just outside my open window.

At breakfast, I learned what had happened. I had made it back to the rooming house, presumably on the trolley, stumbled upstairs in the dark, and then scared the hell out of my mother by barging into her room and falling down on what I thought was my bed. Startled, she screamed, waking up every guest on the floor. They came out of their rooms to shake their heads at me as my mother guided me next door where I belonged.

The story became a family joke, one that was told at family gatherings along with the creaky stories of my father in Ireland and my mother meeting him at a church carnival right after a fortune-teller predicted that she'd meet a dark-haired man from across the ocean.

"That's our Kieran," Mom or Dad would say.

One of the Best Days Ever

I went back to New Orleans two years later, just before I graduated from high school. This time I was accompanied by my drinking buddy Jerry and a friend of his named Dave.

We were driving Jerry's grandmother's car, a brand-new Chrysler 300 convertible, a true muscle car wasted on an old lady who never drove over the speed limit. We went roaring up the highway, eager to get to the Crescent City where we could get drunk and hoped to get laid. It was the early 60s, when good girls — the girls we dated — never allowed us to venture beyond the Maginot Line that circled their waists.

My brother Kevin's apartment was our first stop. He welcomed us… then warned us about the hookers. Hold on to your money, he told us. Their job is to get every nickel you have before they let you go.

We thanked him, promising to come by again, and then searched the Quarter and its environs for the cheapest digs we could find so we would have plenty of dough left over for the drinking and the whores.

It was already past 1:00 a.m. by the time we checked in and got settled. But this was New Orleans, after all, and the clock would not stop us. We splashed on the cheap cologne Jerry had brought and headed for Bourbon Street.

My first experience of New Orleans had been embarrassing. This time I was going to show the city I loved what I was really made of.

As we walked down the crowded street, I could feel the money, two wads totaling 50 dollars, one folded up in each of my loafers, just in case I got rolled. I don't remember the name of the first bar we went to. Like many of the dives along Bourbon Street, it was dingy, smoky, and smelling of stale beer and urine. There were a few tables and booths — and behind the bar, a small stage where some aging dancer moved listlessly.

We sat in a booth and ordered drinks that were delivered by three women, one for each of us.

Mine — that's how I thought of her, as "mine" — slid into the booth next to me. She was tall and slender with sparse blonde hair and, though not truly pretty, was pretty enough for me in her made-up way. She was wearing a blue spaghetti-strap dress cut so low that I could see the tops of her breasts.

"Buy me a cocktail," she whispered.

Having been cautioned by my brother, I was reluctant to agree to her first pocket-draining demand. I refused.

Without another word, the woman reached up and pulled down the top of her dress, exposing the first pair of real live breasts I'd ever seen.

"Give the lady a cocktail!" I hollered.

I realized later that I had misinterpreted Kevin's warning. The danger wasn't in getting rolled. I didn't get rolled. The danger was in rolling myself. For that's what I did.

I spent the 10 dollars or so I had in my wallet then took the hidden money in my right shoe and gladly blew it on buying her alcohol-free cocktails, just so I could keep those breasts in view. It wasn't until all my right shoe money was gone that I came to my senses. Luckily, I still had money in my other shoe... or I would have missed out on Delores.

They say you never forget your first sexual partner. For me, that was Delores. Delores worked at Norma's on the corner of Dauphin and Dumain, Norma's Cathouse, that is. My two buddies and I made our way there the next evening, drunk on Jax Beer that sold for less than a half-dollar per tall boy, but not so drunk that we'd be turned away. Just drunk enough to, you know, take the edge off.

One of us knocked and the door swung open to reveal my grandmother. Not really. It wasn't my grandmother, it was Norma, the proprietor of the brothel bearing her name. She was portly, gray-haired, wearing jeweled glasses and an evening gown. She looked us over. She nodded and gestured us into a foyer furnished with several loveseats. As I recall, she asked us where we went to school. (Maybe this was some kind of test?)

"Loyola," I said.

She nodded. "It'll be 10 dollars. You give the money to your date."

She reached over to a cord hanging by one of the loveseats and gave it a tug. In minutes, six girls wearing panties and bras marched into the room. The three of us looked at each other, wondering what to do.

"Take your pick," Norma said. "That's the way it works."

One of the girls had dark hair cut in a pageboy. Dark hair and a nice smile. I held my hand in her direction. "I'm Delores," she said. She stood, took my hand, and led me out of the room and up a flight of stairs to a hallway with a row of individual rooms, like a hotel.

On the way up the stairs, she told me she was a college student. Undoubtedly a lie, but one I willingly accepted.

The sex act with Delores was as innocent in its own way as the kiss I'd shared with Ginny Duffy when I was playing Sir Lancelot and she was Guinevere.

"I'm sorry," she said as she closed the door of "our" room behind us. "I'll need the money."

Shaking, I handed her a folded 10-dollar bill.

She slid my slacks down, and I gasped as she touched me.

"Your first time?" she asked.

I admitted it was.

"That's okay," she said. "It'll be fine."

She washed me, playfully, and it was almost more than I could take. But she knew what she was doing. Before I got too excited she led me to the bed. She lay down and spread her legs, smiling at me.

"C'mon," she said. "It'll be fine."

She was right. It was fine. But it was too damn fast. Delores was probably happy with my speedy performance but I wasn't. I tried to take my time getting dressed. I didn't want to have to sit in the foyer and wait for Jerry and Dave.

Again, Delores smiled.

"Come," she said and led me out of the room and into the foyer. When we got there, who do you think was waiting for me? Yup, it was Jerry and Dave, sitting there with stupid smiles on their faces.

It was one of the best days of my life… ever.

MILITARY
MISDEMEANORS

Out of the Frying Pan

One of the advantages of going to the Jesuit high school was that you were virtually guaranteed college acceptance. Even someone with my benighted academic record could get in somewhere because the standards of the school were so high.

But of the 90 students in my senior class, two did not go to college. Jerry, my drinking buddy, was one. I was the other.

Instead, we decided to go into the military. Jerry opted for the Navy. I chose the Air Force.

Because I hadn't yet reached the age of 17 years and 6 months, I needed to get my parents' signatures in order to enlist. And it wasn't going to be easy. My father was furious with me for wanting to turn my back on college. It was an opportunity he'd never had. He told me so. My mother just cried whenever the topic came up.

Dinners were difficult during that time. We sat at the table — father, mother, Pat, and I. But we did none of the usual bantering and arguing. We ate in silence, except for the clinking of silverware against plates, the creak of furniture as one or another of us moved, the muted sounds of chewing and swallowing.

Those meals seemed to last forever. I avoided my mother's glance because the sadness in her eyes was too much for me to handle. I dared not look at my father for fear one of us would say something we'd later regret. I did occasionally look at Pat, and he relieved the pressure a bit by smirking at me. I was taking all the heat now and he liked it.

But my parents' consternation only made me more determined to establish my independence, and thus my manhood, as fast as I could. Finally, I wore them down. Not because they thought my plan had any merit but because they saw the futility of sending me to college where I would surely fail. In June 1962, they signed the papers.

From that day until the day I left, the house was filled with a resentful silence. We, all of us, even Pat, moved like wary animals, afraid to talk to each other. Though I was looking forward to leaving home, I was understandably nervous, even frightened. My parents, too, must have felt something about my leaving, something more than just anger, but there was no way for us to talk about our feelings. In our home, there was no precedent for such conversations.

Finally, just before I left, my father and I spoke. It was exactly what I expected. I could have written the script.

"Well," he said, "You've made your bed. Now you have to lie in it."

I nodded.

He looked away as if he were trying to keep himself from saying the rest of what he had to say. But it welled up and he let it out.

"You've made this decision," he said. "You're on your own now. If you ever need anything, any money, don't call me. You won't get it."

I stood there fuming. I thought about the time he'd let me drive his car to a job interview. He was terrified I'd have an accident — not because I might get hurt, but because of what it would do to his car.

"If you have an accident," he'd said, "just keep on going. Don't call me. And don't come back here."

Until then, I had always taken that as a joke. Now I wasn't so sure.

The next morning, I left on a bus headed to Jacksonville and the induction center.

Into the Fire

Looking back now at the nearly five years I spent in the Air Force, I feel like I'm watching a film that is running at four or five times normal speed. The people and events blend together in a bewildering mélange. I have memories — many — but they are fragmented and unfocused. I'm not even sure about the time sequences, not at all.

Did I go from San Antonio to Mexico when I was in Texas for the first time, or the second? When, exactly, did I get run out of town by a Mexican sheriff? Did I truly sell medical morphine to a black marketer — I know I sold booze and smokes and Base Exchange radios — or is my drug dealing a story I heard from some guy or read in some book or simply dreamed up, a lie told so often that it became the truth?

I remember the night I spent in Jacksonville before I was sworn in, let loose at the bus depot with orders to report to the recruitment center in the morning. My last chance to run, but I didn't. Instead, I, we, the six of us who rode north together, flocked immediately to a pool hall we spied, a smoky pool hall with a sullen black man racking balls and a counterman willing to sell cheap wine to teenagers, probably to watch us stumble. It was Mogen David — affectionately known as Mad Dog 20/20. I loved the taste of it, thick as honey, sweet as a kiss, and loved it even more for the kick that made it the drink of choice of alkys everywhere.

I played pool for the first time that night, losing a five-spot to a beardless hustler, and then settled in for some drinking. Somehow, I ended the night in a fleabag hotel, 17 years and 3 months old, trying to pick up a hooker about 40 years my senior, her lips a red gash cut in a face as gray and wrinkled as an old handkerchief. I asked her if she wanted a drink and she said she wanted Thunderbird. I had to ask her what it was. She just looked at me and started singing like a madwoman:

Thunderbird, how's it sold?

Good and cold.

What's the price?

Thirty twice.

It was what I would come to recognize as the Thunderbird jingle, sung in honor of the rotgut that was sold for 60 cents a bottle to the lowest of the low-bottom drunks.

I bought us each a bottle and we drank in her dirty room, sitting on an unmade bed. She wanted to trade sex for money, but I was unwilling to pay even though she said she'd wrap those wrinkled lips around my cock.

I left her room, forgetting that I'd rented my own, and I ended my first night of adult freedom on the sidewalk with an empty wine bottle between my legs.

In the morning, I made it to the recruiting center just in time to weave into a sterile room filled with folding chairs, an American flag, and a bald senior master sergeant. I raised my trembling hand and swore allegiance, vowed to protect America from enemies both domestic and foreign — and had no idea what I was doing and gave no thought at all to the words I was saying.

From there, my fellow recruits and I hopped a plane bound for Texas — Lackland, the busiest Air Force base in the world.

Basic training was pretty much the way it is in the movies. A tough drill instructor with a heart of gold screamed that we were shit. Then, later, he made sure we wrote home to our mothers. We — there were 64 of us in a "flight" — were a disparate group of young men, teenagers really, most from the south but with enough New York and Philly and Boston blood to make it interesting.

For the first time in my life, I became familiar with black men — actually black boys my own age. We were reluctant friends, uncertain of each other's motives. But as we were all suffering under the same oppression, we had a lot in common. This was before Black Power, before Selma, before Dr. King and Jesse Jackson, back in the time when the races didn't mix, even when forced to live together, as we were.

Our days were long. Close order drills, inspections, G.I. parties to clean the barracks, KP, deadly boring classes to teach us how to become good airmen, more KP, and after about four weeks, a quick run through an obstacle course. Then a parade and promotion to Airman Third Class, one step up from Airman Basic.

In the middle of basic, Spring Hill University in Mobile, Alabama notified me that the Jesuits who ran the school had decided to let me enroll as a freshman. Since I hadn't applied, I presumed it was the result of some last-ditch effort on my mother's part.

It was tempting, but I didn't bite. Maybe I'd go do college someday — but first, I intended to have some fun in the military.

From basic, I went to a technical school in Mississippi for about eight weeks, training to be a medic. My only clear memory of that time is of a night spent drinking 3.2 beer in the airmen's club, then picking up a big corn-fed gal from Iowa and sneaking off with her to roll in a patch of long, fragrant, damp grass, not getting laid but getting chased back to the airmen's club by an air police truck that shone a spotlight on our frantic non-coupling.

Later that same night, drunk of course, I got into a fight. My antagonist was a good ol' boy from Georgia who outweighed me by 50 pounds. He said something to provoke me and we went at it. It got ugly. There was a furnace of anger inside of me that I had not recognized before. It fueled me to beat this big boy's ass. I broke his nose by slamming his head against the bunk, and I did it over and over again until he started to cry.

That was not the last fight I had as a serviceman. There were many others. But it was the only one I clearly remember. Perhaps, like fucking, the first one sticks with you.

From Mississippi, I was shipped west, back to Texas, to a technical school that was to prepare me for duty as what the Air Force called an "aero-medical tech." All I remember of those days are the times I spent standing in formation on a long-abandoned landing strip, marching and marching and, as often as possible, fleeing south through the barren country that lay between the air base and the border towns of Del Rio, Texas, and Villa Acuna, Mexico.

The bridge across the Rio Grande led to a world where I could drink as much as I wished — and not just 3.2 beer but real beer and tequila and Jack Daniels and other drinks I'd never heard of. And, of course, there was the sex. So much sex that I could smell the damp fecundity as soon as I entered Boys Town, the red-light district that lay just outside Villa Acuna.

Boys Town was a roughly triangular area, formed by three narrow streets fronted by one bar after another, tiny shacks with women standing in the doorway and offering blow jobs for a buck... around the world for two bucks... any possible sexual activity I could dream of at bargain basement rates.

There was an off-limits section along a dirt street, an extension of the triangle's base, which we were told was just too dangerous for gringos. Needless to say, that's where I headed, to a bar with an honest-to-God hitching post out front. I slouched in and ordered a *Carta Blanca, por favor*, grinning as I nodded to the dark, short, chaps-wearing *caballeros* who turned to glare at me, then smiled when they realized I was just a harmless, foolish gringo drunk.

I met an American woman there, a former teacher, she said, now working as a whore because it was what she wanted to do. I had a poem in my pocket that I'd written about the pimply hills of South Texas and I showed it to her. That's when I discovered the power of poetry.

She read my poem and stuck it inside her bra. Then, later, she took me to her bed, free of charge. In the gray dawn, we walked from Boys Town into Villa Acuna proper and had eggs in a dirty restaurant. I fell in love with her, not the last time I'd fall in love with a whore. And though I never again saw her, booze and sex were now twisted together in my mind even more than they were before.

Months later, I was picked up outside the bar by three wild men in a Caddy convertible. The back seat was crowded with cases of cold *Carta Blanca* and we drank and sped south, roaring along and laughing. The car's shocks were so shot that when we'd hit a dip or a rise in the road it would start rocking, from front to back, the bumper hitting the ground and spewing sparks that could have blown us all to hell and back. It didn't faze me.

I left them in a parking lot outside of Boys Town and learned later that day that they'd beaten and robbed some prostitute and almost got killed. A few days later, I was sitting in the cowboy bar, having a beer, when a big, fat guy sat next to me and lit a cigarillo. He had a greasy mustache and a sweaty belly pooched out over a bullet-laden belt holding a pair of white-handled pistols.

"You with those ol' boys in the Caddy?" he asked.

I nodded.

"They got theyselves in a heap of trouble."

I told him I'd already heard.

"I don't think you're one of 'em," he said. "But I don't know. So here's what. I don't want you in my town. Don't let the sun set on you in this here town. If you do, I'll bury you so deep in a Mesican jail" — that was the way he said it, *Mesican* — "I'll bury you so deep your mama and daddy will die not knowing what happened to you."

It sounded like dialog from a bad movie, but he clearly meant business. I thanked him for his consideration, finished my beer in a gulp, and headed north, back to the base.

I Fall for an Ugly Old Broad

Gretchen was blonde, beautiful, and wholesome. Why she dated me in high school, I never understood.

I dated her to get back at Joe, my nemesis. I saw them together at the senior prom, and it made me crazy to see him with such a beautiful girl at his side. Monday morning, I cornered him in the school parking lot and found myself telling him that I could have his beautiful blonde girlfriend in the back seat of my car in two weeks if I put my mind to it.

Those were fighting words and we fought. He threw me on the ground and then lay on top of me, smothering me into submission. That made me even angrier. I swore to myself that I would make good on my threat.

I called Gretchen that very night and asked her out. I muscled up the courage by reminding myself that even if she said no, she'd likely tell Joe and that in itself would piss him off. But she surprised me by saying yes. I didn't expect much from that date, but we got along. She seemed to like me. I asked her out again — still telling myself that I was doing it because of Joe. (And he was fuming!)

Before long, I had to admit to myself that I liked her. And though Gretchen was not the kind of girl to let me get her in the back seat of my car, that was okay. Joe would never know that for sure.

When I joined the Air Force, she and I had been dating for just a few months and we both knew it wasn't serious. A straight-A student, she was going to college and I was going into the service, a move that typically was made by guys with no future to speak of, a way to avoid unemployment. Still, while I was in training, she and I wrote pretty steadily. I carried her picture in my wallet and we talked on the phone a few times.

I'd managed to finish medical training near the top of my class and, as a consequence, was given my choice of assignments. I volunteered for a two-year tour of duty at Tachikawa Air Force Base, about 30 miles outside Tokyo. This was a plum job, one of the best in the service. It was in an exotic, distant location, a location I would almost certainly never visit on my own. I'd often thought about how exciting it would be to be transported to a whole new world, to see sights that only a few Americans had ever seen —

and this was it. I decided that I would write about my experiences, maybe in a book or maybe in a series of newspaper articles.

Since I'd be stationed in Japan for two years, I was given a full month's leave to go home before I had to report at Travis Air Force Base in California. During that month, Gretchen and I started dating again. And I found myself falling in love with her. That wasn't difficult considering how beautiful she was. With her long blonde hair and blue eyes she looked a bit like Sandra Dee, one of the actresses I idealized in my fantasies.

I hoped my going overseas would convince her to spread her thighs for me, but it didn't. We did spend hours, though, rolling around in the front seat of her car in an agony of incomplete coupling, with her whispering entreaties for me to stop… stop before we did something we'd regret forever.

There it was again, that clear dividing line between "good" girls like Gretchen and the whores who worked the streets of Villa Acuna or, for that matter, the "easy" girls, usually unattractive and not very bright, who let themselves be fondled and more for the price of a movie or a hamburger. Good girls, Gretchen-like and chaste, were to be honored and respected, enabling young men like me to feel good about ourselves even as we spun slowly in the wind, hung with a noose of what we thought was sinful desire.

And so, I spent almost my entire leave with an erection and what used to be called blue balls.

My time was so focused on Gretchen that I hardly did any drinking while home. Of course, I was still only 17 years old and in a state where drinking was limited to adults over the age of 21. A couple of times, I stopped by a bar where I'd heard the bartender wasn't real keen on checking IDs and managed to get a pretty good buzz on. But that was about it.

And, so, in mid-December of 1962, I climbed aboard a jet and flew to Los Angeles, and then took a bus north to Sacramento, a short distance from Travis Air Force Base. I had a little time to do some sightseeing in Sacramento, so I took a cheap hotel room near the downtown, fully intending to visit a museum or two.

As I checked into the hotel, the busboy asked if I wanted a bottle or anything else. That was all the prompting I needed. Forget the sightseeing. Forget museums. Bring me a bottle of vodka and let me get loaded.

Reeling down the hall, I ricocheted from one wall to the other on my way to the lobby. I plopped myself down in an overstuffed chair and was almost instantly approached by an aging hooker with the worst case of bad breath I have ever experienced. We gravitated to a nearby dirt-floor dive, where we drank and talked business. And I was falling in love with her just because she was willing to let me fuck her.

Less than 15 minutes later, nestled between the old broad's flaccid thighs, I thought about Gretchen. But it was not Gretchen I wanted. I was drawn to ugliness and darkness and danger. However much I had the chance to enjoy the opposites — light and beauty and decency — I never could hold on to them for very long.

It would be years before I recognized this as a pattern. That I would do almost anything to ruin a good thing when I had one.

FUCKING – AND FUCKING UP

Glasses Boy-San

I arrived in Japan two weeks before Christmas, after a brutally slow flight on an old C-118 that strained its way from Travis Air Force Base in California to Hickam Field in Hawaii, then on to Guam and, finally, Tachikawa.

My first day on the base was busy with the routine of checking in with the hospital squadron and the flight surgeon's office, where I would work, and getting myself organized in the barracks — a Quonset hut that had housed Japanese pilots during World War II.

My "room" was a partitioned space about the size of a large walk-in closet, separated from a hallway and about 60 other little partitioned spaces by a curtain. And one of the first things I learned about barracks life was that I didn't have to worry about cleaning my quarters, making my bed, shining my shoes, or doing my laundry. For a dollar a week, I could hire a "Momma-san" to do it for me.

As I unpacked my duffel bag that first evening, airmen reeled in, jabbering about their night in Tachi City — the bars they'd drunk in, the girls they'd screwed, and the brawls they'd gotten into. I couldn't wait to get in on the fun.

The next day, after I finished my duties at the flight surgeon's office, I walked about a half mile from the barracks to the main gate that led to the city of Tachikawa. On my way, I stopped in the base airmen's club, a two-story building with a formal bar, a dining room, a stag bar, and game rooms with slot machines and a cashier's window. There I changed my greenbacks into "scrip" that I could use on the base and local currency (at the rate of 360 yen to the dollar).

While standing in line at the window, I told myself that being in Japan was an opportunity to straighten myself out and have a better life. All I had to do was make an effort. Even as I went forward with my debauched intentions, I promised myself that I would.

As I exited the base I felt both happy with my resolve and excited about the evening ahead. I walked along a narrow street, crowded with Japanese locals and GIs and alive with music and aromas spilling from the bars and restaurants that lined the street. It was a bit like New Orleans but more exotic. More dangerous too.

My first stop was a large bar just 100 yards or so from our compound. It was noisy and smoky and filled with possibility — hostesses in skimpy western-style dresses, standing in wait or dancing with GIs. The band was playing "I Left My Heart in San Francisco." Not just once but over and over again.

I had a drink and decided not to have another. There. I left, proud of my self-control, and walked the street again, passing dozens of smaller bars, no larger than living rooms, each serving a handful of customers, each staffed with a handful of girls. In these smaller venues I discovered I could buy large (633 ml) bottles of Kirin beer for 200 yen, about 55 cents, and mixed drinks for the same. A bottle of *sake*, Japan's national drink, cost just over a quarter. A bargain, I told myself.

Two drinks in my belly, I walked the street again, loving the smell of this new town, the cooking meats and vegetables, the smoke from open fires and grills, and the fecund odor from the *binjo* ditch that ran along one side.

My next stop was a flashy, western-style lounge. I stepped in and had a good hopeful feeling. Rock 'n' roll music blared. Kaleidoscopic lights made me dizzy. I was greeted by a truly gorgeous bar girl in a skin-tight red dress. She introduced herself. We had a few drinks. I have a vague memory of pouring Guinness stout and champagne into one of her high-heeled shoes.

I have no memory at all of how she took my money — but she must have, because I didn't have anything left when I awoke in the barracks the next day.

I decided to stay away from the fancy lounges and the gorgeous girls. I figured that way I'd be less likely to drink my way into a blackout. So the next time I went to town, I looked for something small and unpretentious. A tiny place caught my eye. It had about four tables and a bar only about 10 feet long. On impulse, I ordered my first sloe gin fizz. It was good, like fruit juice. I told myself it was safe to drink a few of them.

My next memory is of regaining consciousness in a taxicab, sitting next to a tiny, kimono-clad woman who jabbered on and on in Japanese. The next thing I knew, we were out of the cab and sitting on a futon on the floor of what I guess was her one-room apartment. We were eating chicken wings. I soon figured out that I'd given the woman some money so I could spend the night in her bed. As it turned out, I was too drunk to do anything other than pass out and then get kicked out of her apartment early the next morning.

At first, trying to keep to my resolution to straighten myself out, I only drank myself into oblivion once or twice a week. That was okay, I figured. Plenty of guys did that. To keep myself from drinking more, I kept busy in every way I could.

Before leaving home, I had made arrangements with my hometown newspaper, the *Clearwater Sun*, to file a feature article every two weeks about my experiences in Japan. Though I only earned 25 cents per column inch for the articles, I was making money as a journalist. I considered myself to be on my way to fame as a writer.

I also enrolled in college extension courses and I volunteered to teach colloquial English to Japanese college students who had a working knowledge of the language. That had me traveling by train once a week to a church classroom in the little town of Ocha-no-Mizu, a suburb of Tokyo.

I worked hard at my job. And in my free time, I explored Japan. I boarded trains at the Tachikawa station without knowing their ultimate destination, gave the conductor enough money to get me someplace 10 or 20 or 30 miles away. I walked the streets of Tokyo and Yokohama and Ocha-no-Mizu and cities whose names escape me and let the sights and smells and sounds of the ancient culture wash over me. I loved the people and their impeccable manners, the music, the food, the architecture.

Of course, not every Japanese was friendly. The war and the fire-bombing of Tokyo and the A-bombs were fresh in the memories of many. Once or twice I was spit at, and more often than that I was cursed. It helped that I struggled to learn the language and became comfortable enough that I could carry on limited conversations. I even learned to write a few words in *hirakana*, a cursive alphabet used to write English words, and *katakana*, a phonetic alphabet used by children and foreigners to write Japanese words.

All my ducks seemed to be in a row.

Within three months of my arrival, a sergeant I worked for nominated me for Officer Candidate School, a program that would have earned me a commission. But that wasn't meant to be…

At night, when I didn't have classes or teaching duties, I'd sit in my room and drink cheap beer as I wrote long, aching letters to Gretchen or worked on an abysmal sci-fi novel that bore a remarkable resemblance to *The Day of the Triffids.* And I was going down to Tachi City at least once a week and getting drunk. But I was better with that. I didn't take a lot of money with me on those jaunts and that forced me to take it easy, though it's a lousy way to drink.

It worked until I got a letter from Gretchen confessing that she'd met a guy at college, slept with him, and decided it was time for us to "take a break" from one another. That tore me up. Not only was she was dropping me… she'd screwed that Joe College guy after all those times she'd pushed my sweaty little hands aside, left me groaning in frustration.

"Hell," I told myself, "I'll show her." I headed for town with a new sense of purpose, wanting to get drunk and laid and not giving a damn about the consequences. I pushed my way through the cluster of old whores who always gathered outside the main gate. I kept walking till I found the smallest, dingiest bar on the strip. I wanted to do my drinking in a dive.

I remember nothing more of that night. But I do remember waking the next morning next to a woman who was at least 60 years old, maybe 70, with only two or three teeth and a broad grin. We were in a tiny house on a futon set on a beautiful *tatami* floor of woven reeds.

A television was burbling on a small lacquered table in one corner.

"Do to me again what you did last night," she mumbled. Her English was actually very good, but it was distorted by her lack of teeth.

"What?" I asked.

She spoke more slowly. "Do to me again what you did last night."

Oh, my God, I thought. I didn't want to do whatever it was again. I looked around for a way to escape. I shook my head.

"I like you, Boy-san," she said. "You move in here with me, yes?"

"Okay," I said. "I'll run back to the base and get my stuff. You wait here. I'll be right back."

I grabbed my shirt and shoes and scurried out the sliding door, running toward the base and safety. As it turned out, it was only a partial escape. For several weeks, every time I'd leave the base (and I did almost every night), I'd find her waiting just outside the gate.

As soon as she saw me, she'd perk up and start calling to me. "Glasses Boy-san," she'd chirp.

"Why you no come back to see me, Glasses Boy-san? Why you no buy me drinkee?"

I'd just keep walking, not looking at her, pushing my way forward as she trotted after me in her kimono, her *geta* (sandals) clattering against the cobblestones. I'd shake my head and she'd troop noisily after me.

"Why you shake neck, Glasses Boy-san?" she'd cry. "Why you shake neck?"

Years later, I heard a speaker at an AA fellowship meeting say that he woke up one morning with his arm around a woman he'd never seen before, a woman so ugly that, in his words, he didn't know whether to wake her or chew his arm off at the shoulder. I identified. And as I looked around that meeting and saw all the men and women laughing and nodding, I realized how common an experience that is for alcoholics, even for hard drinkers. I know now, though, how little those lunatic couplings had to do with sex and how much they were a response to loneliness. No wonder I was willing to sleep with an old hooker. No wonder she was willing to sleep with me.

I've laughed to myself, more than once, thinking that, at that very moment, in some meeting of the fellowship somewhere in Florida or Chicago or somewhere else in the world, a woman (or, hell, maybe even a man, I can't be sure) was telling her (or his) story and talking about the time she (or he) woke up next to some drunk named Kieran, a guy so nasty she (or he) didn't know what to do.

"Waking up next to him was my bottom," I imagined her (or him) saying. "From that day to this, I've never taken another drink."

For me, Gretchen's letter opened the floodgates. My resolve to better myself crumbled. It would be almost 20 years before I willingly went to sleep fully sober.

I drank every hour of the day that I wasn't too sick to drink, locked up in a mental ward, confined to a treatment center, in jail, or in prison.

I drank to experience the sheer joy of drinking. I loved it when the switch would click and I'd suddenly feel whole and healthy. Then, as time passed, I drank to survive, to quiet the shakes, to still the voices, to ease the pain. There's no joy in that Mudville, trust me. Calming the sickness is a miserable, full-time job.

Smoke in Eyes

The Bar K was one of the least noticeable joints on the strip, not much larger than a studio apartment, the dirty mirror behind the back bar festooned with Christmas lights and stained photos of San Francisco and Hawaii. The music came from a cranky record player that squawked only two songs: "Take Five" by the Dave Brubeck Quintet and "*Shiroi Hana*," a mournful Japanese number about the loss of love in cherry blossom time.

Like all the bars in the area, it smelled of smoke and booze and waste from the unisex *binjo* with its open hole over a pit emptied regularly by untouchables driving what the GIs called honey wagons. The manager was an old man, tiny, wizened, crude, called "*Oto-san*," or "Father," by the four or five girls who worked the bar, cadging for drinks, taking men home for money, giggling together like the schoolgirls they were.

The bartender — everybody called him Johnny though his real name, as far as I was able to determine, was Shoji Yamamoto — was a slimy character, complete with gold teeth and oily hair. Of indeterminate age, but certainly old enough to have been an Imperial soldier in World War II, he spent most of his time behind the bar trying to steal from soldiers and airmen who got drunk enough not to pay close attention to their money. He and I liked one another and enjoyed playing a card game much like baccarat. We partnered up and cheated the unsuspecting patrons.

I spent hours in the K, drinking Kirin Beer and *sake* and cheap booze by the gallon, spending money I didn't have, running up a tab of hundreds of dollars on pay of about 100 dollars a month. I ate my meals in the bar, fell in love in the bar — first with Nobuko, who looked on me with something like pity from her perch as the most popular of the girls, then with Aiko, a tiny, tragic sexpot who spoke no English and left after about a week.

In my insanity, I decided to search for her across the city from the Air Force base in a part of Tachikawa that was off limits to GIs. I found her, briefly, in Tachikawa and then heard she was working at a bar in Tokyo. I followed her there and was standing on a flight of stairs talking to her when her boyfriend, a teenage *yakuza* — a member of a violent gang — pointed a pistol in my direction. I scrambled down the stairs as fast as I could, ran to the train station, and left the city, pretty sure that I could survive without Aiko.

After Aiko, I fell in love with Yoko, a country girl with a country girl's love of drink and food and laughter. She spoke enough English and, by that time, I spoke enough Japanese that we could converse, and we started spending time together after the Bar K closed for the night. We spent night after night drinking together and then sleeping together.

It took a while for me to get used to the idea that when she was working she had to flirt with customers, pay no attention to me, and occasionally agree to meet men after hours. When that happened, I would go to the train station and wait. She would show up a little later, laughing and showing me the money she'd earned. Usually, she and I would go to a hotel that seemed as old as Japan itself, walking along narrow streets under ancient trees with me loving the sights and smells of the country and the sounds of dimly heard music, not jazz or rock but music that had been played for 1,000 years or more.

On her days off, we visited Tokyo Tower and went shopping and ate sushi. We said the words I love you back and forth but it was part of the script we had to follow. I knew she was unhappy when we talked of love because she cried every time she got drunk, remembering some boy in her hometown of Nagano.

Drink was central to our time together, both the drinking itself and the sobering up. One November morning, I was lying on a futon with Yoko in a small hotel in the town of Ocha-No-Mizu. We'd been drinking the night before and somehow ended up screwing and sleeping there. It was early, just before sunrise. I was smoking, Yoko was sitting up, ready to slip back into her kimono. She turned on a radio by the side of the bed. Suddenly, the quiet morning was broken by a man almost shouting in excitement. He spoke so fast all I could understand were the words "*daimyo* Kennedy" repeated over and over.

Yoko looked at me, her eyes wide and her mouth open. Slowly, her voice low, she told me President Kennedy had been shot in Dallas and that he was dead. When she said Dallas, it sounded like *Darrass* and I wanted to laugh but I couldn't. I knew I had to get back to the base.

As I walked to the train station, the few people I passed stopped and bowed. I boarded a train headed to Tachikawa and the car was crowded — but as I entered, people backed up, moved away to leave a space around me. Their faces were solemn. Several bowed toward me. I heard men and women murmuring words I didn't understand and I saw several weeping openly and unashamedly. I realized, suddenly, that they were expressing their grief at the death of Kennedy and allowing me the room to grieve without interference.

The last time I saw Yoko was on New Year's Eve. She met me in the Bar K, dressed in a white silk kimono embroidered with pale pink flowers. Tiny bells in the heels of her *geta* tinkled each time she took a step. We sat and drank *sake* and she called me Kieran-chan and I called her Yoko-chan. We laughed and drank glass after glass. At midnight, I kissed her, first the back of her neck beneath her upswept hair and then her mouth, tasting warm *sake* on her tongue. I told her I loved her and she looked at me and she was weeping. I didn't know if it was for her old boyfriend or because she sensed that this was to be our final night together. I asked her what was wrong and she laughed a laugh she didn't mean. "I'm not crying," she said, as if reading a line from a bad movie. "It's smoke in eye." And then she laughed again.

In the morning, dressed in her favorite black-and-white kimono, she announced that she had to visit her family. I walked with her to the train station. I was happy to be with her, hopeful for our future. We stood on the platform, saying nothing, watching the train pull in. We kissed. I fondled her hair and she climbed aboard. As the train pulled out, she lifted her hand and waved.

A Near-Nympho
Alcoholic Bar Owner

When I returned to the Bar K a few days later, nobody seemed to know where Yoko had gone. It seemed odd, the way everyone denied any knowledge of her whereabouts.

Weeks passed and I knew that I would never see her again. I figured she went back to her hometown to be with her old boyfriend.

One night, sitting on my usual stool at the back of the bar, looking down at my hands or at my glass, a woman I'd seen in the bar before, a woman named Takeko, slid onto the stool at my side. Johnny had told me that she worked on base as a secretary, which made her the only non-bar girl I'd ever seen in the K. She was pretty but fragile looking, skittish, as if she'd run for cover if you made a quick move in her direction. I knew from watching her drink that she was no lightweight. Her hands trembled slightly as she picked up her first drink, probably the first drink of her day since she came in about the time a daytime shift would have ended on base. She drank straight shots of vodka and tossed it neat, without a grimace or wince.

That night we began our drinking together. We ate too — fried gyozo. And then we drove to her house in her car, a tiny Renault. She had vodka, plenty of it. We drank and talked. I was feeling good. But then we started talking about our past lovers and I told her about Yoko... and she laughed at me.

"What's so funny?" I said.

"Do you really think Yoko left town to go back to her old boyfriend?"

"Yes," I said. "That's what she told me. And why would she lie?"

Takeko laughed again. "Because she was probably pregnant with your baby. She had to get away from you so she could get rid of it and get on with her life."

That made more sense than the boyfriend story, and I felt like a fool. I was furious.

"I don't believe it!" I yelled, and slapped her hard. She slapped me back and I grabbed her arms. We fell to the floor and my anger turned into something else. We ripped at each other's clothes and made love almost savagely.

And when we woke the next morning, we were still twined together on the *tatami* floor.

From that day until the day I left Japan almost a year later, Takeko and I were lovers. She was, in many ways, my ideal lover. Older by almost 20 years, she was shy in bed, as she was everywhere else, but also as voracious as if she were discovering sex for the first time. And that's not all. Turns out she was part owner of the Bar K.

I didn't find that out until I'd pretty much moved into her house and we walked into the K together for the first time. I ordered drinks for us both and asked Johnny to put them on my tab. He looked at Takeko. She told him, in English, to bring her my tab, a folded piece of notebook paper kept in the register. When he handed it to her — it must have been about 200 dollars — she looked at it for an instant, tore it into pieces, and put them in an ashtray.

Johnny just smiled and nodded at me the way he did whenever I got a particularly good hand in one of the card games we played.

From that night on, I didn't have to think about money. Though I continued to run a tab, it never seemed to amount to more than 10 dollars or so. When Takeko wanted to go out for dinner or drive to Yokahoma to spend the night, the money appeared. And if there was something I wanted to buy for myself, she would buy it for me.

More important, I loved the fact that Takeko drank like I did. Often, we'd sit together in the K until 10 o'clock or later, then drive to the base where she'd buy a bottle of vodka at the Civilian Club, where she was a member. Back at the house, we'd pass the bottle back and forth, swigging, until it was empty or we passed out or we decided to stumble off to bed to make love. She always made sure the alarm was set.

There's an old line that the best girlfriend for an alcoholic is an alcoholic nymphomaniac who owns a bar. Takeko was not a nymphomaniac, but she was close enough for me.

Before Takeko and I met, I engaged in small, tawdry, nickel-and-dime crimes. The kind of crimes that net what is known as "chump change." I stole from the men in my barracks, money and small items I could sell or pawn. Sometimes, at least before I met Takeko, I stole because I needed money to drink, to pay my tab at the K, but other times I stole simply because I could get away with it. A time or two, I stole when I was drunk just because I could and I wanted to.

I didn't just steal, I operated, for a time, in a very amateur way, on the fringes of a flourishing black market. The authorities tried to control the black market by issuing ration cards that could be used to buy four cartons of cigarettes, four bottles of booze, one radio, one camera, etc., each month. I overcame that obstacle by paying non-smoking, non-drinking men in my squadron a small fee to make purchases for me using their cards.

I bought cigarettes at the base exchange for about a dollar a carton and sold them off base for 5 dollars. I bought Johnny Walker Red on base for about 3 dollars a fifth and sold it off base for 25 dollars. I have a vague memory of stealing a package of four morphine syrettes from the flight surgeon's ambulance and peddling them for 200 dollars in a bar in the off-limits sector of Tachikawa City.

I was a petty thief, and not a very good one at that. A shrink might say I wanted to get caught because I made few efforts to hide what I was doing. I openly talked about making money on the black market. And, of course, I did get caught. I was arrested for stealing a camera from a fellow airman — a camera I pawned using my military I.D. card as identification. Because I was young — still just 18 — and because I had no record, the judge advocate took it easy on me at my court martial. I was sentenced to 30 days in the stockade and stripped of my two stripes.

I was able, somehow, to convince Takeko that my arrest was a mistake, that I was innocent. She came to visit me on the weekends, bringing cigarettes and candy. I never brought up the crime I'd committed and neither did she.

When I was released, my time on base was understandably miserable. No one wanted me as a roommate, so I lived in an empty corner of a large barracks, an area that had been damaged in a rainstorm and never repaired. At night, when I was unable to go off base, the other men made fun of me as they passed, laughing about the sneak thief, the fucking punk, the loser.

I was also unwelcome in the Flight Surgeon's Office where I'd worked before my arrest, so I was put to work washing ambulances or cleaning the hospital kitchen or, most often, filing the thousands of lab slips that were generated by the hospital every day. And, of course, I drank as much and as often as I could, alone if I had to.

There were some good times, though, always with Takeko, always away from the base. Once, to celebrate my 19th birthday, we traveled to Yokohama and spent the weekend in a hotel overlooking the bay, stuffing ourselves in a Chinese restaurant that Takeko said was the most famous in Japan and drinking ourselves into near oblivion in a waterfront tavern.

She gave me a watch for my birthday. I lost it somewhere that night but neither of us seemed to care.

Not long after that, we went to Kamakura so I could meet her mother, father, and younger sister. It was late winter, and snow was falling as we drove from Tachikawa south and slightly west to the ancient city that had served as the de facto capital of Japan during the Kamakura Era. As always when we were together, we were drinking, even as we drove the roughly 40 miles along the Japanese coast.

We stopped at a bar in downtown Kamakura and sat for hours drinking *sake* and Suntory whiskey and eating red caviar on crackers. It was late afternoon when we finally made our way to the house where Takeko's family had lived since the end of the war. It was high on a hill with a view of the *Daibutsu*, the Great Buddha statue that had overlooked Kamakura Harbor for almost 1,000 years.

The house, a traditional Japanese home, was small. The main room was furnished with a large, low table, a lacquered breakfront, a television set, and a charcoal burner for heat. Just off the main room were sleeping rooms, a dining room, and a kitchen. As Takeko and I entered the house, we took off our shoes to protect the *tatami* floors that were woven from white straw and bordered with red silk.

Her father, Takeko had warned me, was not fond of Americans. He bowed shortly in my direction. I bowed more deeply as a sign of respect. He and Takeko spoke rapidly back and forth, phrases bursting from their lips like machine gun fire. Takeko's mother, old and shrunken, dressed in an informal kimono, flitted nervously around the edges of the conversation as Takeko's younger sister (we'd met once in Tokyo) knelt silent as a statue in the corner. Finally, Takeko's father, I called him *Kikuchi-sama* to show respect, snapped an order in his younger daughter's direction.

"Get the *gaijin* a knife and fork," he said, using the moderately insulting word for foreigner that put me in the position of being a potential enemy. I wasn't fluent in Japanese, but I understood. Bowing again, to show I meant no insult, I answered in Japanese.

"*Haashi* will be fine," I said. "I know how to eat with chopsticks."

The old man's eyes widened. I realized I may have been the first American he'd met who knew even rudimentary Japanese. He looked from me to Takeko and back to me. Then, bowing, he indicated that I should join him.

For the next four hours, first in the main room and then the dining room, the old man and I drank Suntory, Japan's only single-malt scotch, and ate a meal I can't much remember, and talked the best way we could, a mix of rough English, rougher Japanese, and sign language. At some point, he hauled out an old, worn photo album and showed me pictures of men and women in kimonos, standing in front of temple gates, hotels, houses, boats, and cars.

The pictures were, except for the clothing, exactly like the pictures in my parents' albums. Then he flipped to one of a young Japanese man, standing in front of what looked like a Zero, the famous Japanese fighter aircraft. The man was smiling into the camera, his eyes narrowed against the sun. The old man looked at me without blinking. He looked down at the picture. He slammed the book shut and poured us both another drink. I remembered Takeko once telling me, in passing, that her older brother had died in the war, shot down over Iwo Jima.

The whiskey kept flowing and the old man and I were swaying slightly where we sat at the low table. He said something to Takeko, too rapidly for me to catch. Bowing, she left the room. When she reappeared, she was carrying a folded, formal outer kimono, quilted black and thick. Her father struggled to his feet and draped the kimono over my shoulders. It smelled of mothballs, of age.

I ran my fingers over the silk. Takeko leaned close to me. She whispered, telling me the kimono was almost 200 years old and that it had been given to one of her ancestors by the Emperor. She pointed out the five embroidered crests, two on the front, one on each sleeve, and one in the middle of the back.

"My father is giving you an honor," she said. And I knew it.

Eventually, I was shown to a tiny guesthouse, about 30 yards up the hill from the family home. I was so drunk I had to be helped up the path and into what was really just a single room with a futon. I fell onto the futon fully clothed and someone covered me with several quilts. Hours later, I woke with an urgent need to urinate. There was no bathroom in the guesthouse, so I wrapped myself in a quilt and walked onto the porch. I stood there, swaying drunkenly in the cold, urinating into the night, looking down at the ground where my piss marked the white snow.

Suddenly, I became aware of everything around me — the gently falling snow, the dark trees against the slightly lighter sky. I looked down the hill and had a clear view of the giant statue of Buddha... and beyond that, the harbor exactly as it had been a millennium earlier when the statue had been erected inside a temple.

"I'll always remember this night," I thought. And I have. I remember, too, that when Takeko and I got back to the base and she dropped me off so I could change for work, I was arrested on charges of breaking and entering and grand theft.

What Kind of Bird Don't Fly?

I don't really know why I committed the crime that landed me in the stockade for the second time. I know I was drunk when I suddenly got the idea to break into the storeroom behind the airmen's club, but I don't know why I thought it was a good idea. It couldn't have been because I needed money. I could have begged or borrowed it from Takeko. Maybe I wanted to get a couple of free bottles of booze. Maybe I was just pissed at the Air Force or the squadron or some sergeant.

Here's what I do know, or think I know. Sometime after the little club closed that night, I crept from the barracks across the base to the door that led to the storeroom. I remember the snow on the ground and having to put my hands in my pockets because they were so cold. I tried the lock, tried to jimmy the lock with my pocketknife, tried to jerk the door open, and had no luck. If I'd had any real luck, I would have left then and gone back to bed. Instead, I noticed that the door's hinges were on the outside, shining dully in the moonlight. "How stupid," I thought. And using my pocketknife, I pried the pins out of the three hinges that held the door in place, lifted it aside, and leaned it against the wall.

There wasn't much to steal. Just a small pile of the scrip we called "MPC" (Military Payment Certificates), a handful of change, a couple of bottles of scotch that I planned to sell off base, and a roll of chits I could use to buy drinks at only one place: the airmen's club I was burglarizing. I stuffed the loot in my pockets and put the door back in place without replacing the pins in the hinges.

As I stumbled back to the barracks I smiled to myself, thinking how surprised the next person to open the door would be when it came crashing down on his head.

I was proud of myself. Proud even as I realized the drink chits wouldn't do me any good and stuffed them down a sewer grate. Proud even as I realized that my crime netted me no more than 50 dollars. I was proud because I thought I had gotten away with something. Then I remembered that I'd removed the hinge pins and the door with my bare hands, that I'd rifled the cash box with my bare hands, that I'd moved bottles with my bare hands, that, in other words, I'd left fingerprints all over the crime scene. And, of course, the Air Force had my prints on file.

So even as I drank with Takeko's father, even as I looked down on the *Daibutsu* in the snow, I knew my time as a free man was running out. I guess I could have tried to hide, but where could I have hidden in Japan? I was six feet tall and had flaming red hair. All I could do was wait for the hammer to fall.

So that's what I did, and it fell on the morning that Takeko brought me back to base after our trip to Kamakura. Within a few weeks, I had my second court martial, was found guilty, and was sentenced to six months of hard duty, a fine I couldn't pay, and a Bad Conduct Discharge (BCD).

I lived in the base stockade, a group of Quonset huts surrounded by barbed wire. Each day, I'd leave the stockade dressed in a pair of fatigues marked with a large white "P" to show I was a stockade inmate. I'd make my way across the base on a bus, to an office where I'd sweep and mop and clean for eight hours. That was to be my life until my sentence was up so I could be discharged and sent back to the States.

Takeko didn't come to visit, though she did send cigarettes and write me one letter wishing me luck. And her wish came true. After I'd done most of my sentence, I was offered a chance to go through a program that would enable me to go back to active duty and not get a BCD.

I realized that I truly did not want to be saddled with a less-than-honorable discharge, not if I ever wanted to work at a decent job or get a passport or do anything other than be a bum. So I agreed to go to Amarillo, Texas, to the Air Force "retraining school" to be reclaimed as an airman.

The evening of my departure, I dressed in my blue uniform, stowed my gear in a duffel bag, and hopped in the blue pickup truck that an air police-man would use to drive me to the base terminal. I knew we were about three hours early and knew, too, that Takeko would be home from work.

"Listen," I said to him, "I've got a girlfriend off base. I'll never see her again. Any chance you could swing by her house so I could say good-bye?"

When he didn't just tell me to go screw myself, I knew I had him.

"She's a good girl," I said, "not a bar girl. It would really mean a lot to her, and to me."

He nodded.

"It has to be quick," he said. And then he cuffed my hands together. "Just until we get there," he said.

Ten minutes later, we were at Takeko's house. I knocked on the door and heard her moving inside. Slowly she opened the door about halfway. I tried to reach in to hug her but she moved back out of reach. I explained that I had only about five minutes but that I wanted to say goodbye. I told her I'd get my life straightened out and come back to her. I promised.

She shook her head.

"You don't think I mean it?" I asked.

"No," she said. "I don't want you to come back. Just go and leave me alone. I love you, but you are no damn good."

As I walked back to where the air police truck sat idling in the narrow street, I could feel her gaze on my back. Climbing into the truck, I turned and saw her standing there with her arms folded over her breasts, like some kind of shield that would protect her from me. Even from the distance, I could see her face was wet with tears. I raised my hand to wave to her and she shook her head.

We drove to the terminal in silence, my hands cuffed together once again. And as we walked through the narrow building we passed a group of airmen who were just arriving from the States.

"What kind of bird don't fly?" one of the men cackled.

"A jail bird!" another one answered.

The whole group laughed. All I could do was hang my head and keep walking.

JAIL BIRD

My Name Is Kieran
and I'm an Alcoholic

What the hell had I done? I'd truly screwed myself this time. I wanted to cry but just didn't have the energy, wanted to scream but couldn't. I shook my head. "Fuck. I gotta quit this bullshit," I thought. "There has to be a way for me to straighten up, get control of myself, of my life.

I was shuffled aboard a Flying Tiger charter aircraft packed with rowdy Army troops, mostly grunts from the First Air Cavalry Division returning from duty in Korea. I sat in the back of the plane, looking out of place in my blue Air Force uniform.

My seatmate was an air policeman who'd been assigned the job of being my watchdog. He was returning to the States after his own tour of duty.

"You're not going to try to jump out, are you?" he asked as the plane taxied for takeoff.

I shook my head.

"Then I guess we can take the handcuffs off," he said, smiling.

It was legal, in those days, for GIs to carry cheap liquor home from Asia, and it didn't take long after the plane was airborne for some GI to open a fifth and start passing the bottle around. Within minutes, grinning civilian stewardesses — probably veterans of the return flight ritual — were pouring drinks for all the passengers, including me. I don't remember what I drank but I do remember joining in as my fellow passengers boozily sang "When Johnny Comes Marching Home" and a particularly weepy rendition of "I Left My Heart in San Francisco." By the time we were four hours into the flight, almost everybody was plastered, most were asleep, and the cabin was pretty much silent.

It took about 10 hours for the Flying Tiger to get from Japan to our first stop in Alaska, which was still reeling from the March 1964 earthquake. After a brief stop in Anchorage, we headed south to Travis Air Force Base. During the flight I was able to stop thinking about how screwed up I was, able, for a time, to act as if I weren't some small-time criminal headed from one stockade to another.

But as soon as the plane touched down, my seatmate clicked the cuffs into place and hustled me off the plane and into a terminal where another air policeman grabbed me. For the next day or two, I was locked down in the stockade at Travis. From Travis, I was taken — again in cuffs — to a depot where I boarded a train for Amarillo, Texas. For some reason — perhaps they wanted to see if I'd try to run — I was put on the train all alone, with no cuffs, with a ticket for a sleeper and chits to pay for meals.

I made my way to the dining car, empty at that hour, and managed to convince a friendly porter to swap cash for my meal tickets, cash I could spend in the bar car. I was in heaven. Just a couple of hours earlier, I was an airman basic on my way from one jail to another, and now I was sitting comfortably in an observation car, a vodka and tonic in my right hand, a cigarette in my left, imagining I was a famous writer or maybe a spy or a movie star, anybody but myself.

Luckily, I had only enough money to finance a slow slide into tranquility, nonchalance, and warmth, not to get drunk enough to do what I really wanted to do: jump off the train and, like some desperado, head for Mexico where I'd end my life living with a beautiful brown-skinned *señorita*.

The next day, I was sober, broke, and no longer wrapped up in my fantasy. When the train pulled into the station in Amarillo, I was taken in tow and hauled to the air base. My new assignment was to the 3320th Air Force Retraining Group, where I was supposed to morph from an imprisoned, law-breaking airman into a good trooper, law-abiding, willing to shine my shoes and show up for duty sober. It was the job of the retraining group airmen — really policemen — to keep me from wasting my life, giving me a second chance by providing me with healthy doses of group therapy, life skills, and general military chicken shit.

To guarantee success, the powers that be decreed that the time I spent at the retraining group would not count as part of my enlistment and that I could be kept there until it was determined that I was "retrained" and fit to return to duty. In other words, I had an indeterminate sentence that could stretch all the way to infinity.

Part of my retraining required admitting that I might have a problem with booze and attending some meetings of a fellowship of sober alcoholics. I was, of course, still telling myself that I had no such problem — this despite all the evidence to the contrary, including the fact that I was spending a lot of time in handcuffs. I figured I just needed to do a better job of controlling myself.

In those days, the early 1960s, movie stars and rock 'n' roll heroes weren't bragging about their addictions on talk shows and inviting the paparazzi to snap their pictures as they hopped in and out of rehab. Most people knew little or nothing about the few programs that existed. They were the subject of wry jokes that made the shame attached to alcoholism even worse. Indeed, for most alcoholics, the only way to participate in those programs was in disguise, sidling from one shadow to the next, hoping they wouldn't see anybody they knew.

For me, disguise was not an option. One evening, a group of us, maybe a half-dozen, were loaded onto a bus, handcuffed of course, and hurried off base and across the dusty, hot city to a parking lot beside a ramshackle building that looked as if it might at one time have been a restaurant or, I thought with a grin, a bar. Our air police guard unlocked our cuffs and herded us off the bus with instructions not to fraternize with the natives. Instinctively, we fell into something like a loose formation and were led into a grubby hall lined with folding chairs.

We stood together, glancing uneasily at the others who were there — mostly old men, along with a few well-worn women, milling around a coffeepot. As I looked at them, I realized with a jolt that I was far younger than anyone else in the room.

"Jesus," I thought. "I'm only 19. I'm too damn young for this crap. I'm no alky. I just like to drink."

Finally, a tiny little man took his place behind a table at the front of the room and hammered away with a gavel as he hollered for everyone to get ready for the meeting.

The other prisoners and I took seats at the back of the room. Most of the others shuffled their way to folding chairs near the front.

Hanging on the wall behind the table were two lists, one headed "The 12 Steps" the other "The 12 Traditions." Before I had time to read the lists, the little wizened man stopped hammering and shouted, "Hi, everybody! My name is Lou, and I'm an alcoholic!"

There was a brief moment of silence. Then, in unison, the alkys at the front of the room shouted, "Hi, Lou!"

I felt dizzy. Disoriented. Then Lou asked if there were any newcomers in the room. As one, all the alkys at the front of the room turned to stare at me and the other uniform-clad prisoners.

One of us, a balding guy from Brooklyn doing time for punching some staff sergeant, must have been at a meeting or two before because he piped up, "My name is Jerry. And I'm an alcoholic."

"Hi, Jerry!" everybody shouted. "Welcome!" And they started to applaud.

"Holy shit," I thought. "What's this all about? Who ever heard of applauding you for being a drunk?"

One of the other prisoners looked over at me and shrugged. Then he shouted out his name — Fred, I think it was — and said he, too, was an alcoholic. Again, everybody started to applaud.

"What the hell," I thought. I wanted to be applauded too.

"My name is Kieran," I yelped. "And I'm an alcoholic."

Applause rolled over me and it felt pretty good. I was tempted to stand up and take a bow. I thought maybe I'd give this outfit a try.

Then the meeting started in earnest. The little guy led everybody in what I learned was "The Serenity Prayer":

God grant me the serenity to accept the things I cannot change; the courage to change the things I can; and the wisdom to know the difference.

After that he made a few announcements, and then introduced a speaker. For the next half-hour the speaker told his story. He told us how he never felt like he fit in and how he drank to feel comfortable. He told us how he'd lost his job. How his wife left him and he lost contact with his kids. On and on. Then he told us how he'd come to a meeting and surrendered to God and how wonderful his life now was. He was happy, he said, that he'd been sober for one whole year thanks to "the program."

Well, that sounded okay, though I wasn't sure what the "program" was. But the guy sure didn't look very happy. In fact, he looked like he had a corncob stuck up his ass. Even when he smiled, he looked like he had a corncob up his ass. Still, everybody applauded him.

Then he was replaced by a second speaker who basically told the same story — except he said he was happy that he'd been sober for three years, thanks to God and "the program."

A woman was next. I was hoping she'd tell us how she gave a lot of blow jobs to get drinks, but all she did was tell pretty much the same story... except that she was happy for five years of sobriety.

The problem with all of these speakers was that they looked as if they needed a good stiff drink. The whole room was dingy and sad. To my mind, a couple of bottles of booze would cheer things up.

The guy sitting beside me, a New Yorker with a strong Brooklyn accent, leaned over. "If my choice is staying drunk or going to silly meetings like this and telling people stuff about myself," he said to me, "there's really no choice. I'm just gonna stay drunk."

"Me too," I said.

And so I did. For about 30 more years.

The New Girl

During my retraining, I was assigned to the flight surgeon's office where I cleaned exam rooms, filed papers, and typed. My supervisors paid little attention to me. My colleagues were friendly. The workload was light.

I wasn't allowed to enter the on-base airmen's club and I wasn't allowed off base. So, for the first time in many years, I had lots of free time during which I was sober. I devoted that time to reading and writing.

I tried to write science fiction, took a shot at writing a novel about me and Yoko, and wrote some non-fiction and short stories, all of it pretty terrible. But I was writing more than I ever had and I liked it.

After four months, I was deemed fit for duty. I'd been reduced in rank to airman basic, the lowest rank possible, earning about 70 dollars a month. Still, I couldn't wait to get the hell out of Amarillo and back to a life of freedom.

I couldn't leave until the orders for my new assignment came through, and that would take at least a couple of months. So, I continued to work at the flight surgeon's office during the day and I got a night job at a drive-in restaurant, filling orders in the busy kitchen. For three weeks, I worked both jobs diligently and didn't take a drink. Then, one night, I did.

I told myself I could have a beer and be okay. I'd seen a bar with a couple of pool tables down the road from the drive-in and I was pretty sure they'd serve me without asking for identification.

I was right. That first night, I had two beers and went back to the base. The second and third night, I got a bit lightheaded but still made it back to the barracks without a problem. The fourth night — it was a Friday night — I decided to drink some Thunderbird, the rotgut wine with a kick like a mule.

I bought two quart bottles and headed for a park across the street from the drive-in. I found a place to sit under a tree, well out of sight. I didn't want was to get hassled by the police. I leaned against the tree and drank the cold wine, grimacing from the taste but loving the way it felt, that "click" that made my eyes water and made me grin.

I stayed under the tree until sometime after midnight and then got up and started walking to the base. The street was nearly empty, and I was sure I'd make it back without getting into any trouble. Yet there was something heating up inside of me that made me sad and angry. I spotted a fire hydrant with a metal chain, about the same size as a dog collar, hanging from its top. For no particular reason, I grabbed the chain and yanked on it until it pulled free. I wrapped it twice around my fist and walked on, weaving slightly, until I came to a small shoe store, dark and empty. Still walking, I swung my fist at the center of the store's display window and then jumped back as it shattered into shards and blades and slivers of glass.

An alarm sounded. I ran. Four blocks from the store, I ducked into an alley. My hand was bleeding. I was scared. Just ahead, I saw the lights of a gas station and walked there as fast as I could, holding my hand out to keep the blood off my clothes.

Nobody paid any attention as I hurried into the men's room. Luckily, I only had one cut across the knuckle of my middle finger and I was able to stop the bleeding by pressing a paper towel against it. I heard a siren approaching. I held my breath till it faded and was gone. "Holy shit!" I thought, looking in the mirror. "What did I do?" And then I was laughing.

I sat down on the toilet and stayed there for almost an hour before someone pounded on the door.

"One minute," I hollered.

I ran the water in the sink for a few seconds, then left quickly and hitchhiked back to the base.

About a week later, a new girl came to work at the drive-in. She was about 18, chubby but cute. I made friends with her. She told me she had just moved from a small town in south Texas. From the way she talked, I got the impression she was a runaway.

I took her to a movie one night and then to the park where I'd gotten drunk on the T-bird. She kissed me shyly. She wouldn't let me touch her breasts. But she stroked my cock and then put it in her mouth. All the time her eyes were shut.

The following week was her birthday. I promised her a surprise. I took her to dinner at a nice place not far from the drive-in. She ordered trout and they served it to her whole, head and all. She looked at it like she was going to be sick. She sipped a Coke and poked at the fish while I had a few drinks and teased her about it.

After dinner, I took her to a cheap hotel. She was silent, completely silent, as I undressed her. She wore old-lady panties, about as sexy as a crutch. I didn't care. I took her hand and led her to the bed.

As I entered her, she closed her eyes, just as she had when she'd sucked my cock. When I came, she started weeping. I got up, went to the bathroom, and cleaned myself. When I returned, she was still in bed crying. I began to dress.

"I have to go," she said in a whisper.

"Okay," I said. "You want me to go with you?"

"No," she said. "You just stay here."

She dressed in silence. I watched. She left without saying goodbye. I knew I'd never see her again. It didn't bother me at all.

A Hell of an Idea

After six months in Amarillo, I finally got my orders to go back to active duty. I had roughly two years left on my enlistment, and I was assigned to the flight surgeon's office at Webb Air Force Base in Big Spring, Texas. It was a base and city that made Amarillo look like the Garden of Eden. I had some leave time accumulated, so I decided to go home for a bit first.

My parents had pretty much given up on me, knowing I'd been in the stockade and then the retraining group, but they let me sleep on the sofa in their apartment at the motel and fed me and tolerated me while I was there.

My first night home, I borrowed my old man's car so I could go out on the town. He told me what he always told me whenever I drove his car: "If you have an accident, don't come back. Just head for Canada and keep going."

With those words ringing in my ears, I drove from Clearwater Beach across the tree-lined, landscaped causeway to the mainland, looking for action. Clearwater then was more a small town than the vacation spot it is today. Teenagers, and I was still one, spent hours driving from the beach to downtown, then along the main street to an always crowded and noisy hamburger joint across from the high school. Once around the hamburger joint's parking lot, then back on the main street to go "around the horn" — back to Clearwater Beach and back to town, over and over, looking for girls or a drag race or a fight or whatever.

There was a football game at Clearwater High that night. I walked to the stadium, not because I wanted to see the game but because I wanted to see if I knew anybody in the crowd. Cigarette smoke hung over the stadium like hazy layers of fog in the overhead lights. For a moment, I stood just outside the end zone, looking up at the stands, searching for a familiar face but not really expecting to see one.

"Kieran. Is that you?"

I turned and started to laugh. Patti Dornbos — my old girlfriend from junior high was standing with a friend, grinning. She looked the same as when I'd last seen her, gorgeous, with long hair, flashing brown eyes, and those amazing breasts. We hugged.

Over the next few weeks, I spent almost all my time with Patti. A few times, when she was busy, I went to a bar where they didn't pay much attention to ID cards and I sat and drank enough to get a buzz on. My mind, though, was on Patti. We went for long drives and spent hours in an all-night diner just off Main Street.

We talked and laughed and talked some more. She was enrolled at the local junior college, studying to be a dental hygienist, and we talked about her future. We talked about what I'd do when I got out of the Air Force, about my plans — I made them up as we were talking — to go to college, get an advanced degree, and become a college professor.

One night, late, we sat in a gazebo in a tiny park overlooking Clearwater Bay. She took my hand and led me to a grassy spot. We made love. It was rushed and awkward. I was drunk and dizzy. Still, I managed to lift her skirt and crinolines (yes, crinolines), remove her panties, and do it. It was wonderful, I thought.

The next day, she skipped school and took me to her bed in her mother's house, and by the time I had to return to Amarillo and then report for duty at Webb Air Force Base, we were talking about getting married. I was still 19, going on 20. Patti was 18, going on 19. I had no money. I was once again an airman basic, a no-striper. I had no real future. We had no business getting married except that we were in love. We hoped that would be enough.

I took a bus from Amarillo to West Texas, arriving a day early so I'd have an opportunity to get drunk before starting my new job. I don't remember where I went or what I did. All I remember is that I woke up in a hotel the next morning and I could find neither my hat nor my dress shoes. I had a vague recollection of throwing them away but no idea why I'd done it.

When I finally made it to the base, I was hatless and wearing a pair of faux alligator slip-ons, hoping I'd be able to lie my way out of trouble. I knew as soon as I walked into the hospital squadron's administrative office that it wasn't going to be easy. The office itself was tiny, the living room of a small mobile home, in the middle of which sat a young second lieutenant. He looked at me and asked me about my get-up. I told him someone had swiped my hat and shoes when I was asleep on the bus.

He shook his head. "I think I should give you an Article 15," he said, referring to an option in the Uniform Code of Military Justice that would allow him to punish me for a minor offense without going through a court martial. "What the heck," he shrugged, "you already got no stripes. You're already screwed up. Just report for duty."

"Yes, sir."

He told me where the barracks was and where the flight surgeon's office was located.

"Am I going to have trouble with you, airman?" he asked.

"Oh, sir, no sir, sir." I said.

"I hope not."

The lieutenant had told me that my reputation had preceded me, and, as a consequence, the only one he'd been able to find who was willing to have me as a roommate was a guy named David Carrero.

As I walked to the barracks with one of the company clerks, I asked him what David Carrero was like.

"You'll see," the clerk said.

When we got there and I pushed my way into my assigned room, I couldn't believe my eyes. Though the men are permitted to display a few personal items, barracks rooms are always decorated in strictly military style, with green walls, green curtains, single beds made up with olive-drab blankets, everything ship-shape. The room I entered was neat, but not very military. It had white walls and a Turkish carpet. A half-dozen sketches and several oil paintings hung on the walls and a wine bottle with a candle in it sat on the desk in front of a double window.

"You two should get along as good buddies," the clerk said as he turned to leave.

While I was unpacking my duffel bag, my new roommate walked in. He was short, slender, with dark hair and eyes… and was blatantly and un-abashedly effeminate. I was surprised. Keep in mind that in those days, anyone who was even suspected of being homosexual was harassed and, usually, kicked out of the service.

He introduced himself and said he was glad to have a fuck-up as a roommate.

"You're going to hear from everybody that I'm a queer," he said.

I nodded.

"I heard you're a thief."

I nodded again.

"Well," he said, "I am a queer. And I guess you really are a thief. But as long as you don't steal from me, I don't care. And don't worry about rooming with me. Despite what you may have heard, we don't attack other men while they sleep."

I promised that I wouldn't steal from him and he promised that he wouldn't try to get in bed with me — and we honored that agreement.

David ended up being a great friend. One thing he did do was introduce me to the Big Spring Amateur Theatre. He'd been in several plays there, and he talked me into volunteering as a painter, cleaner-upper, and general gofer. Almost immediately I was cast in the play they were working on at the time, *Stalag 17*. I had the part of one of the prisoners-of-war. By the time the curtain fell on opening night, I had fallen in love with the idea of acting, being the center of attention, and hearing applause. During the balance of my time in Big Spring, I acted in one play after another.

When Patti came to visit during school breaks, we'd stay in a motel that sat right at the end of the air base jet runway. We'd lay in bed together, talking or making love, and as an F-104 or a T-38 screamed just 100 yards away or howled low overhead to make a landing, the whole room would shake, with dust falling from the ceiling and the window air conditioner threatening to fall out.

We were there on Christmas Eve. We had put a tiny tree on top of the television set in our room and were drinking a gallon of foul-tasting muscatel. It was the first time I saw Patti get drunk. She'd only had about two glasses of the wine, but she started crying, telling me how beautiful the tree was. She fell asleep and I carried her to the bed, then I passed out on the floor.

One of us should have known, have foreseen, that that scene — with me drunk on the floor while Patti slept alone — was a pretty good forecast of what lay ahead for us. But neither of us gave it any thought. And so Patti went back to Clearwater and school, and I lived in the barracks and we wrote and talked on the phone.

And then, on June 6, 1965, Patti's 19th birthday, I came up with a hell of an idea for celebrating it. We got married.

WIFE ONE OF FOUR: MARRIED AND DRUNK

Starting to Slide

Patti took a break from school so we could live together and we moved into a tiny apartment — a bedroom, living room, bath, and a kitchen so small only one person could stand in it at a time. The apartment was atop a garage and smelled slightly of gasoline.

I was paid twice monthly, about 80 dollars every two weeks, and that included my extra pay as a married man. Even in 1965, it wasn't a lot of money. We made do as best we could. Our meals were simple and our entertainment consisted of going to a local movie theater where we could get in for a buck. Sometimes, right before payday, we had to eat tomato soup made of catsup and water or onion soup using onions I'd find in the trash behind a grocery store.

I drank whenever I could, which was not often given our lack of money. When I drank, I drank cheap wine and got as drunk as I could as fast as I could. Patti would have just a glass or two of the wine and get a little giggly, but she never seemed to think my drinking was out of the ordinary or worthy of comment. Perhaps it was the times and our surroundings but it seemed that our friends — other young servicemen and their wives — drank pretty much the way we did. I never missed work because of my drinking and I had no trouble with the law, so I simply thought I liked to drink a little more than most other people.

After about six months, we moved into a rickety old farmhouse close to the base, a place the owner let us occupy for free just to keep it safe from vandals. With no need to pay rent, my drinking increased.

We bought a used television set for 10 dollars and an old record player and we'd invite friends to the house for impromptu parties. They'd bring wine, and we would sit around listening to Bob Dylan and Joan Baez, the Mamas & Papas, drinking and making big plans for the future. In the evenings and on weekends, I wrote poetry, terrible poetry, and made believe I was a beatnik. But I reported for duty every weekday morning and even got a couple of promotions. I saluted when I had to and said "yes, sir" and "no, sir" and conformed in every way.

About six months before I was due to get out of the service, Patti left me alone in Texas and went back to Clearwater so she could finish school and get her license as a dental hygienist before I came back to civilian life. The plan was for her to work while I then went to school. By that time, I'd done a fair amount of acting at the Big Spring Amateur Theatre and I was interested in teaching theater at the college level.

We rented our free house to a couple we knew. Part of the deal was that I could occupy one of the rooms. That meant I had money to drink whenever I wished. More than once, I showed up for rehearsal at the theater so drunk I could hardly walk, and a couple of times I performed while I was barely able to remember my lines.

In the summer of 1967, almost five years after I'd signed up for a four-year enlistment, I was released from the Air Force. It was an amicable separation. I dumped my uniforms on a garbage heap outside the air base and headed home to Florida.

Patti met me at the airport. We rushed to a one-bedroom apartment she'd found on Indian Rocks Beach, a little town on an island south of Clearwater, and fell into bed. It seemed to us both that our lives were finally on some kind of track. Patti had a job as a dental hygienist. She didn't love it, but she was making enough money for us to live on. I intended to get a job, save the money I earned, and use it to get a degree in theater arts.

For a brief period of time, things weren't bad. Patti was beautiful and sexy and smart and we were starting a brand-new life after being apart for more than six months.

The only job I could get was in an orange juice processing plant in Dunedin, a couple of miles north of Clearwater. Patti's mother worked there as a secretary to the boss and she somehow arranged to get me hired. She must have done it because she hated me. I worked six days a week, from 7:00 a.m. to 7:00 p.m. with a half-hour for lunch and two 15-minute breaks. The pay was $1.65 an hour, with no overtime.

My job was to pack boxes with quart containers of orange juice. A machine spewed the containers of juice down a ramp to where I stood. I grabbed four quarts at a time and slapped them into a box. As soon as the box was filled with 12 containers, I slid it further down the line to another worker who picked it up and stacked it on a trolley. The machine had a tendency to jam and when it did the containers piled together, splitting and spewing juice, so much juice that it pooled around the machine six inches deep, sometimes deeper.

Orange juice is acidic. It eats the stitches out of work boots, not to mention what it does to your feet. I had to buy two pairs of boots in two weeks.

One day, I turned to the guy working down the line from me and made a joke about my old man and my grandfather being union men.

"I should give Jimmy Hoffa a call," I said. "He'd shut this son-of-a-bitch down in about 10 minutes."

I was joking. I didn't know Jimmy Hoffa and neither did my dad. But the overseer who heard me didn't know I was joking. I was given the bum's rush. Hustled out the plant's front door and told never to return.

I felt bad for about two days. Until a friend told me about a job opening at a tourist spot called the Palm Pavilion. Built in the heyday of the Florida boom as a casino, the Pavilion had evolved into a restaurant, gift shop, miniature golf course, and beer counter that ran along the beach. The pay was higher than it had been at the orange juice plant and the work was pleasant. I was dressed in shorts, a T-shirt, and flip-flops, and many of our customers were young women in bikinis. Best of all, I could sneak cans of beer from the big coolers behind the counter.

For the next year, Patti worked at the dentist's office and I worked at the Pavilion. I was drinking heavily almost every day, but I wasn't falling down. I floated through my days on a river of beer. After work, I'd drink at home or Patti and I would go to a beer and wine joint that had pool tables and a jukebox that rattled the windows.

Patti and I got along. I was faithful and so was she, as far as I know.

I had gotten Patti interested in acting, and several times we acted together in productions put on by the Clearwater Little Theater. We also talked a lot about my dream of turning my love of theater into a career as a college professor. Often, when I was working at the Pavilion, cooking burgers or packing beer coolers, I imagined myself wearing a tweed jacket with leather elbow patches, impressing a pony-tailed, plaid-skirted co-ed with my knowledge. She would spread her thighs wide atop my antique desk but I would deny her. Then I would go home and sit in my book-lined den and drink brandy from a snifter.

I imagined I could be an academic Thin Man, drinking martinis for breakfast, always witty and urbane, attending cocktail parties at the college president's mansion and slaying the other guests with my brilliant repartee. Never, not once, did I consider a future spent bent over toilets, puking, wetting my pants, in hospitals or detox centers or behind bars.

I applied to two schools, the prestigious Goodman School of Drama at the Art Institute of Chicago and the University of Milwaukee. Patti looked into getting licensed in Illinois and Wisconsin. I had relatives in Chicago, but, assuming we'd wind up in Milwaukee, we made arrangements to temporarily stay with John and Nancy Leopold, friends from our time in Texas who lived near the university.

The night before we were to leave, I went drinking by myself. I don't remember much of the evening though I do have a clear recollection of walking along the beach, broke because I'd spent all my money in some bar, looking for a car I could burglarize so I could get my hands on some change and get more to drink. I found an unlocked car, parked on a side street, with a purse clearly visible on the front seat. I reached drunkenly inside, snatched the purse, and staggered off.

There wasn't much money in it, just a couple of dollars, but enough to buy a few more glasses of beer. So I headed back to the bar, lurching down the middle of the main street. I'd only gone half a block when a police car pulled up behind me, its blue lights flashing. I panicked, thinking they had seen me steal the purse. Instead, I was arrested for public intoxication.

In the morning, Patti came to the police station and paid my fine. I was chastened by her angry silence and convinced that, at any moment, the police would tie me to the burglary and come looking for me. As we packed our car, a Porsche roadster I'd been able to buy for a song, and even as we drove out of town, I kept looking over my shoulder. Finally, when we were driving north on Highway 19, leaving Clearwater behind, I was able to relax.

"Thee-Tah" Person

When Patti and I left Florida so I could get a theater degree, we had no idea it would be the beginning of my journey down the Jellinek curve...

Every alky who's ever been in treatment or detox has seen this curve in one of its many incarnations. It's always displayed somewhere in the break room, close to a coffee pot or maybe on a refrigerator door. The counselors and nurses and docs who work in these places call it the Jellinek curve in honor of the man whose research it was derived from.

The first time I saw it, on a poster in the alcoholism ward at the veteran's hospital in St. Petersburg, I laughed. "That ain't me," I thought.

The poster showed, with a bold line, the predictable shape of an alcoholic's life. The left side of the curve is a descending slope — from normalcy (a house, a job, a family) to incarceration, institutionalization, or death. Along this downward sweep, symptoms and behaviors are listed, a perfect litany of ruin: blackouts, work and money troubles, tremors, early morning drinking, obsession with drinking, binges, loss of work and family, and on and on until the drinker is in a place where escape seems impossible. The right side of the curve shows how an alcoholic's life may improve if he's able to stay sober. It starts with the simple action of resisting drink for a single day. And then it moves upward, one day at a time. Slowly, very slowly, the alky may start to bathe, eat regularly, go to the bathroom like a normal person, sleep normally, get and keep a job, and regain the confidence of his family.

I laughed at it back then but, as far as my life is concerned, the Jellinek curve was remarkably accurate. Looking at it now, my only criticism is that its description of the bottom is not vivid enough. It's not just the threat of prisons or asylums. It's the loneliness, sadness, rage, bewilderment, despair, and even madness that become part of the undulating pattern of the drunk's life. At bottom, death is attractive, promising welcome relief.

But as Patti and I drove from Florida to Wisconsin, we had no idea about Jellinek's curve and the journey we had really started. Yet, one by one, each of the miseries Jellinek predicted entered our lives. But my refusal to acknowledge the danger I was in was actually a blessing. Had I known what lay ahead for me and for Patti I might have killed myself.

John had told me I'd have no trouble finding a good job in Milwaukee. I figured he might even give me a cushy job working for him. What I wound up with instead was a minimum wage job washing dishes in a French restaurant. On my third day, I got into an argument with the owner about whether or not I could take a bite out of an untouched duck with orange sauce that he wanted me to throw away.

"You simply can't do that," he said with the hauteur only a Frenchman can project.

"Why not?" I said. The damn duck was sitting as pretty as can be on a plate I was meant to wash. "It's a beautiful piece of meat," I continued. "It would be criminal not to eat it."

"You will eat at the end of the night with the rest of the help," he told me.

"Right," I said. "Bologna sandwiches, thank you very much."

"You should apologize," he said sternly.

I turned my back to him. "That guy's fucking crazy," I mumbled, just loud enough for him to hear.

So that was the end of that job. For the rest of the summer, Patti and I survived on a variety of part-time, low-paying jobs. For a week, I sold vacuum cleaners door-to-door. My selling skills were terrible. My only near-sale came on the last day of my first week in training. The prospect was a teen-aged couple about to get married. I gave them the whole sales pitch. I could see they couldn't afford the 300 dollars to buy the vacuum — but that sales pitch! It and been honed and polished by pros and it worked. The husband-to-be was about to sign his name to the contract… but as he picked up the pen, I pulled the paper off the table and tore it up.

"You don't need this," I told him. "You can get a perfectly good vacuum cleaner somewhere else for 10 or 15 bucks.

The money I earned for my week of training — 75 dollars — ran out soon enough. Then Patti and I both went to work selling encyclopedias door-to-door. We were selling education, our trainers told us. We were helping ordinary, working-class people have a better life. But they referred to these people as "mooches." And our sales tactics were even harsher than those

I had used to sell vacuum cleaners. We were part of a team of salespeople who junketed together from one small town to another, trying to avoid local cops since — despite the good work we were supposedly doing — the public view of us was that we were crooks. One dollar of every sale was put into a "fine fund' we could use to get out of jail if we were collared for doing business without a license. Neither Patti nor I ever got busted, but I did get punched in the nose by an angry construction worker who couldn't see the value of a 400-dollar set of books he probably couldn't read. We quit after that.

Meanwhile, Patti took and passed her licensing exams in both Illinois and Wisconsin. And I got word that I'd somehow earned the right to audition for admission to the Goodman School of Drama.

When I'd applied to Goodman, I had no expectation of being accepted. It was affiliated with the world-famous Art Institute of Chicago and was considered to be one of the best drama schools in the country, right up there with Yale and even with Lee Strasberg's Actor's Studio. I was a guy who barely got out of high school and drank his way out of the Air Force.

The day before my audition, I drove to Chicago and spent the night with my uncle Vincent and his family. The next morning, I took the subway downtown. I was early, so I had time to take a quick walk through the Art Institute first. As I ran up the broad, steep steps of the museum, dressed in bellbottom jeans and a cast-off West Point cadets overcoat, my hair below my shoulders, my head bobbing to music nobody else heard, I felt strong and capable — even invincible. I was ready and able to take on whatever life had in store for me. Passing through the museum's doors, I nodded cheerfully at the security guards and then strutted through the galleries, passing canvases painted by Monet and Seurat, bronzes sculpted by Henry Moore, mobiles created by Alexander Calder, and the working models for The Picasso — the artist's controversial (Was it a dog? A baboon? A woman?) "gift to the people of Chicago."

I was confident. I was proud. And I felt I deserved to feel proud. But by the time I got to the audition, I was filled with doubt and fear.

I had chosen the famous "St. Crispin's Day" speech from Shakespeare's *Henry V* as my reading and sang "Try to Remember" from *The Fantasticks*. My performance was weak. My voice broke. My hands were visibly shaking. Yet somehow, I was accepted into the school.

I should have been exhilarated. But I could not accept the idea that I was good enough. I decided that the school must have had some quota for veterans. I was ashamed. On top of the shame, I was worried because Patti and I were broke. Having earned very little over the summer and with expenses for drama school looming, we were forced to beg for help from my uncle Vincent. He hardly had to be asked. Though he had six children, he immediately made room for us in his home and made us feel welcome.

While we were living with John and Nancy in Milwaukee, I was rarely able to buy anything to drink. Even cheap wine was usually out of range. But Vincent ended the drought.

Vincent was a rare breed — a successful Republican state representative in Cook County, Chicago, the home turf of the Daley clan and a bastion of old-school Democratic politics. He was also a wheeler-dealer and a savvy pol who greased wheels for his backers, never missing an opportunity to shake hands. He had contacts, Democrats and Republicans, throughout the state of Illinois. While Patti and I were living in his house, he and I sat up every night drinking quarts of Meister Brau from cases hauled home from a nearby package store by his youngest son in a Red Rider wagon. He'd tell great stories, laughing at how he played the political system and arguing with my liberal views, and we both knew it was all a game.

Our life seemed to change, to fully morph, in a matter of weeks.

Patti found work in a suburb north of the city. For the first time, she had a job she really enjoyed. I applied for and got GI Bill benefits — and I was becoming part of a world I'd never imagined in Clearwater or when I was in the service. We were financially better off than we'd ever been and it seemed as if I was on my way, finally, to a meaningful future.

We found an apartment on Chicago's north side, close enough to Wrigley Field to hear the cheers when the Cubs scored a run and the groans, an all-too-familiar sound, when they made an error or the other team scored a run.

I loved Goodman. I soon became part of a circle of students who were, for the most part, older and a bit more serious than the younger ones. Kip Mortonson, a San Francisco native with the longest, straightest, blondest hair I've ever seen on a man, was in our circle. So was John Henderson, a gifted actor who had just finished a couple of years at Yale's drama school.

There was Billie Mack, one of a handful of blacks in the school, and a guy named Mark who was brilliant but terminally ill with an incurable and virulent cancer. I grew my hair even longer and grew a mustache — threw away my bottle-green blazer from Sears and my rep ties.

I took classes taught by Dame Eugenie Leontovich, the famous Russian actress who had studied with Stanislavski, and by Charles McGraw, who had directed Dylan Thomas in *Under Milk Wood*. I was surrounded by talented people from the theater school and the Art Institute itself. I talked theater, acted a walk-on part on the main stage in the equity staging of *Caesar and Cleopatra* with Murray Matheson, and stood in the wings watching James Earl Jones roar his way through *Othello*.

Drinking was a part of that world. There were cast parties several nights a week where everybody drank and most everybody got drunk. Jones, a star since his performance in *The Great White Hope*, showed up at several of the parties, dressed in shorts and a Cubs cap, ready to sit on the floor and drink beer with the guys and answer questions about his life and acting. Len Cariou, a three-time Tony winner who'd played Iago to Jones's Othello, was more reserved — but, then, he was a Canadian. I circulated on the periphery. I couldn't quite take myself seriously as a "thee-tah" person. I could imagine myself teaching or writing, but I sure as hell couldn't imagine myself as a famous actor, or even a not-so-famous one. Still, it was fun. Patti and I threw parties and were invited to parties.

I drank every day when I was home from school. Somehow I managed not to drink during the day when I had to go to class or rehearse. And I was doing pretty well. Theater history and acting lab and voice offered few challenges. I ranked at the top of my class, or second behind John Henderson, in every course other than dance. I seemed destined for success.

Then, I found Brown's, a tavern on Wabash Avenue, within walking distance of the school. It sold a lot of beer and wine to a clientele largely comprised of postal workers, many of them black men and women. It served great cheeseburgers and had one of the world's best jukeboxes. At first, I'd join John and Billie and Kip and Mark at Brown's for lunch. We'd have a few beers and gossip and laugh and then we'd go back to class. One day, though, I decided to stick around after lunch. I didn't feel much like going to class. So I stayed. And then I stayed more often and longer and longer.

Still, I made it to class often enough to keep my grades up, skipping only a few classes a week in a school where nobody much bothered with anything as mundane as attendance. In one class, theater history, I was given the assignment to design a production of *Macbeth*, working with a costumer. As soon as the assignment was handed out, a girl named Julie cornered me in the hall and asked me to partner with her. She was flaky, always dressed in feathery hats and a boa, thigh-high boots and leopard-skin-pattern pants. But I needed a costumer, so I figured what the hell.

We took the elevated train to her apartment, which wasn't far from mine. The train was packed as it pulled out of the Loop, headed north. We stood close. I could smell her perfume, and even though her damn feathered hat was tickling my nose, my cock stiffened. Patti was at work. My time was my own. Though I'd been faithful to her so far, I was thinking that it wouldn't be difficult to get this girl in bed. I'd take off that goddamned feathered hat but I'd leave the boots on.

Once we were in her apartment, Julie wasted no time. She got us each a glass of wine and when I tried to talk about *Macbeth*, she held up her hand to stop me. She told me that the reason she'd asked me over was because she had a roommate, a girl named Linda, who liked me and wanted to meet me.

I was flabbergasted. Nothing like that had ever happened to me. After a moment, Linda came out of the back room. She was tall, almost as tall as I was. She was slender. Dressed in a pair of suede bellbottoms and a T-shirt, she looked almost boyish, her breasts small, her features fine. Her hair, blonde, shoulder length, was so straight it looked as if it had been ironed. We talked and drank some wine and smoked a little hashish and then I went home and ate fried chicken with Patti.

The next day, Linda and I spent the afternoon and evening in bed. I got home after midnight. I ignored Patti's questions about where I'd been. A week later, I walked out on her. I didn't even talk to her about it. I just left a note on the kitchen table telling her I needed to get some "space" and "think." I moved in with Linda and I drank and we made love and listened to the pigeons that cooed on her windowsill every morning.

I try to recall what I felt when I walked away from my marriage, leaving a beautiful young woman, a woman who loved me. I don't remember feeling guilty. I don't remember feeling much of anything. Like the experts say, alcoholism is a disease of selfish self-centeredness — a degree of self-centeredness that allowed me to leave my wife, a woman I said I loved, for another woman and not think even once about the consequences for her or the woman I was going to screw or anybody else.

A long time later, at a meeting of sober alcoholics, a guy who'd lost his job as a vice president of a large bank told us that when he was drinking, he had "followed a hard dick into places he wouldn't go behind a loaded shotgun." I knew exactly what he meant.

During semester break, Linda and I took off for Indiana with John and Mark and Kip. Mark's father was headmaster at a military boarding school there, and because they were on break too, the school was deserted, empty except for a caretaker. We squatted in Mark's parents' house, a mini-mansion, and drank and smoked a lot of dope and ate wonderful meals using food from the headmaster's pantry.

Linda and I reveled in each other's company — but even as we spent hours in bed and hours drinking, I started to think that I wanted to return to Patti. It wasn't that Linda and I couldn't have stayed together. In fact, she was pressing me for some real commitment. Not to get married, but for me to at least say I wanted to be with her. But I couldn't do it. It seemed like too much trouble to go through the hassle of leaving one woman just to take up with another. If I'd been asked what I felt, I would not have been able to answer. The whole affair with Linda, the trip to Indiana, the fucking and drinking, all seemed outside the action of my own life, being played out on stage with me as the only member of the audience.

It would be easy, too easy, to blame it all on liquor but I can't. For one thing, I was not always so drunk that I didn't know what I was doing. My capacity for drink seemed astounding. I could drink almost nonstop and achieve only a feeling of mellowness, of rightness, without being anything close to incapacitated. While I was at Goodman, with Linda, starting to make Patti's life miserable, starting to destroy my own life, my tolerance grew to a point where I could drink a case of beer or more a day without displaying overt signs of drunkenness beyond slightly slurred speech and a tendency not to remember events that occurred late in the day. I was drunk, make no mistake, and often stoned on the marijuana we all smoked, but I was able to hide it from people who didn't know me well.

I didn't think of anyone but myself. All I was concerned with was getting my needs met, no matter how sick those needs were. As usual in those days, my reason for doing just about anything was that it seemed like a hell of an idea at the time.

So, having hurt Patti in my desire to be with Linda, I then hurt Linda by going back to Patti. At least I had the decency to say goodbye to Linda to her face.

I timed my return by making sure I arrived at the apartment while Patti was at work. I jimmied a front window and snuck in like a thief. I crawled into bed, zonked out, and woke to find Patti sitting on the bed next to me, crying and asking why I'd gone and why I'd come back.

I told her I knew I'd made a mistake. I blamed it on pressure from school. I promised her I'd cut down on the drinking. I swore it would never happen again. And Patti let it slide.

The Breakfast of Champions

Sometimes when I'm at one of the meetings I go to so I can stay sober, I find it necessary to talk about my marriages. I often refer to my wives by number. It's easier that way. Wife number one... number two... number three (a marriage so brief, I barely remember it)... and my current wife, wife number four (though I always call her by her name — Lynne — when I'm with her). When I refer to a wife by number, people usually laugh. I usually laugh. But it's not funny.

After I returned to Patti, our relationship was different. We lived as if we were in two different cities. We acted as if I'd gone on a drinking sabbatical with friends, something that may have been unwise but not a threat to the marriage. Patti was unable to face the truth about my drinking. She retreated into some place where comfortable denial was possible and I was happy to leave her there.

I expressed remorse because it was expected of me. And I wish I could say I hated myself for the way I was living my life, but I didn't. I smirked. I laughed at the people who cared. But it took drink to smirk. It took drunkenness to continue to hurt people I loved. So I drank more and faster.

I went back to Goodman, went to classes, nodded at Linda when I saw her in passing, and drank. I drank beer at home in the morning, then drank whiskey at lunch. I went to classes drunk — and after school, John Henderson and I drank beer until he fell to sleep on our sofa. Then I crawled into bed next to Patti, who was already asleep.

Though I didn't realize it at the time, there was something different about my drinking. It's not that I was drinking more than I had before — it's that it had reached a point where it had become more important to me than anything. A shot of whiskey, a can of beer, a bottle of cheap wine, gave me happiness that nothing else could, not my wife, not my work, nothing.

I'd wake up feeling as if some insane bastard had driven a heated railroad spike deep into the base of my skull while a rat had crawled into my mouth to sleep. I had to force myself to eat. And then one day, I stopped eating. All I needed was the drink.

"Beer? For breakfast?" Patti asked.

"It's just like cereal," I said. "Made from grain."

She shook her head. I drank my beer.

Linda was through with me, but I had a brief and nasty affair with Miriam, a girl in my theater history class. I continued my daily forays to Brown's and other taverns near the school. For the most part, I drank beer or wine, not because I didn't want hard liquor but because it was too expensive.

Drunk as I was, I was still able to keep my grades up. Goodman's culture was helpful. So long as I made an effort to come to class and completed the infrequent out-of-class assignments, I was okay. I acted infrequently and not very well, but that was fine with me and with the school since I had made it clear that I wanted to be a director and writer. They understood that I had no desire to act.

Near the end of my first year, I was in a speech class, drunker than usual, feeling nasty, when the instructor said something I didn't like. I registered my complaint and then told her I thought the whole idea of speech class was idiotic. As a future director, I said, I only needed to speak well enough to give directions. In response, she said something else I didn't like. I hit her. She tumbled back over a desk. My hand was aching. I stood over her for a moment, barely conscious of what I had done, and then ran out of the room, hearing the cries of my fellow students behind me.

The next day, I was kicked out of Goodman. It could have been worse, I remember thinking. They hadn't had me arrested for assault.

Big Shot!

In the 1960s, Kroch's & Brentano's was the biggest, most successful bookstore chain in America. It was also the employer of choice for college dropouts who figured working in a bookstore would have a certain intellectual cachet that couldn't be achieved by washing dishes or begging for change.

Carl Kroch, the owner of the chain, was smart enough to realize that this gave the company the ability to hire bright young people at rock-bottom prices. Within a few days of leaving Goodman, I got a job as a warehouse worker at the main Kroch's store on Wabash Avenue in Chicago's Loop.

I was paid 60 dollars a week to fill phone orders from store managers around the Chicago area. On my first day, I was put to work with an older man, Bill Casey, an obviously smart and diligent guy. Over the next few days, he showed me how to do our job efficiently while we talked about books.

I understood why I was working for minimum wage but it confounded me that Bill, who was at least 50 years old, was stuck in an entry-level position. One morning, I asked him about it. He looked at me skeptically and he said he'd explain over lunch.

When we took our lunch break, Bill led me down Wabash Avenue to a nice restaurant. He led me through the dining room and into the bar. The bartender greeted him and asked if he wanted "the usual." He nodded. Then he asked me what I'd have. I told him "the same."

He brought us two Manhattans. I had never had one before.

Bill explained that he was a new hire at Kroch's, that he had been lured away from B. Dalton, another major bookstore chain. He had been offered the job of vice president in charge of satellite store operations. He was, he said, spending several months working in different departments to get a feel for the company.

I was impressed.

Bill told me that he liked me and thought I had potential. He said that if I stuck with him, he would see to it that I had a good future with Kroch's.

We sat at that bar for several hours, drinking together and talking and the more we drank, the more I liked the idea of working for him. He was a nice man and a successful man. And he knew how to drink.

Bill was true to his word. Within a few months, I was an assistant manager at a store on LaSalle Street and, within a year, the manager of the store on Michigan Avenue. My ego, already irrationally pumped up, had been given a psychological shot of steroids. But rather than imagine the progress I could make in my career, I thought about all the ways I could take advantage of my heightened position.

As luck would have it, there was a bar next door. I found I could zip over for a quick drink and be back before anyone noticed I was gone.

For a while, I did good work and enjoyed my new freedom. I bought a couple of expensive (for me) suits and a handful of silk ties and some French cuff shirts and even a few pipes and some good tobacco — the trappings of the intellectual I saw myself as being. I carried a fountain pen. I read book reviews so I could talk intelligently about the books we sold. Things were going well.

But my visits to the bar got longer. And the attention I gave to my job got shorter. I began a teasing affair with a hippy girl who worked in paperbacks. She would come to my office on some pretext and we'd make out on the sofa. When the Cubs were playing, I was at Wrigley Field or in the bar watching the game on television.

Before long, my paycheck was insufficient to meet my needs. So I began stealing from the store. I told myself that I was being underpaid and the money I took was the least the business could do for me.

My modus operandi was simple. Each day at 10:00 a.m., one hour after the store opened, I cleared the register as if it was the end of the day. Any receipts, and they ranged from just a few dollars to a hundred dollars or more, was my take. Then, with the register reset, it was business as usual. The money the store took in between 10:00 a.m. and closing was Carl Kroch's.

For a time, everything was wonderful. I hardly had to work and when I went to the main store, I was treated like a big shot. I had a key to the executive bathroom and entree to the climate-controlled room where the rare books were housed. When I met with any of my few bosses, I was sober.

I found a skid-row bar in a building not far from work, a place that opened before dawn, a gin mill where a shot of rotgut cost 30 cents, 35 cents with a beer back up. It was there that I drank each morning, two shots, maybe three, sometimes four, before I walked the few blocks to the bookstore.

I started writing again and thinking of myself as a writer. I wrote terrible poetry and prose. When I wasn't writing, I was reading or napping. So long as my office door was closed, my employees knew I was not to be disturbed. There were a few occasions when someone from headquarters would drop in to pay me a visit only to find I was missing. My employees made excuses for me. They knew that so long as they covered for me, I'd let them continue to goof off as well.

The end came in the wake of the publication of Jacqueline Susann's potboiler *Valley of the Dolls*. Kroch's had purchased several thousand copies of the book on the strength of prepublication chatter. My store had a display of 100 copies, maybe more. I hated the book, thought it was tawdry, not up to my lofty standards as a writer who never wrote anything other than gibberish. One afternoon, I was informed that Jackie — Miss Susann — would be in my store the next day for a book signing. Drunk, as usual, I hatched a plot.

Early the next morning, I moved all the copies of her nasty book into our storeroom. Then I waited, standing at my post behind the main cash register. At noon, a limo pulled up. The car's rear door swung open and Miss Susann stepped out, wrapped in mink, carrying a handful of poodle. She swept into the store and straight to me.

"I'm Jacqueline Susann," she said. "I'm here to sign copies of my book."

I tried to look bemused. "What did you say your name was?" I asked.

"Jackie Susann," she snarled.

"And the book?" I asked.

She turned red. "Why, *Valley of the Dolls*, of course," she said.

I acted as if I'd never heard of it, though it was, at the time, at the top of every bestseller list.

"Wait a moment," I said. "Let me run down to the storeroom and see if we have any in stock."

Without a word, she stormed out of the store, sniffing with disdain, her poodle whimpering.

Within an hour, Carl Kroch was on the phone, ordering me to report to his office. I was put on notice. Later that same day, Bill Casey and a phalanx of bean counters descended on the store and ran an audit. Roughly $10,000 was unaccounted for.

I had no idea I'd stolen that much. I also had no defense. Told I had to take a lie detector test, I drunkenly climbed on my high horse and refused. "How can you question my honesty!" I huffed. And I meant it. I didn't act insulted, I was insulted. I quit on the spot.

From Kroch's, I went to work as a janitor in a high-rise building, a job I enjoyed until winter arrived and, in the middle of a blizzard, I had to remove snow and ice from the parking lot. That night, I told Patti I wanted to move back to Florida. She agreed to do it.

Once again, I had a plan. I would go to school at the junior college in St. Petersburg while Patti worked. I thought a new start would get us back on track, that I'd be able to force myself to do better, to somehow drink less.

School for Scandal

I saw her in the cafeteria, just a few weeks after I started classes at the St. Petersburg junior college. She had red hair, freckles, and an impish smile. At 10 o'clock in the morning, I already had a belly full of beer and no fear. I sat down at her table and acted superior and wise, sneering at the book she was reading. She fell for it. She was young enough to think I was a writer just because I carried a notebook and said I was.

She said she'd meet me after her last class. I figured it was a hell of an idea. Her name was Sherri and I fell in love with her instantly.

I had found a bar overlooking the bay where I could sit at an outside table and watch the mullet jump. From midday to dusk, I would drink beer and scribble nonsense in my notebook. Then Sherri would come. We spent most of our time in my VW bus, which I'd outfitted with an American flag curtain and a mattress. We'd park in a field, under palm trees and stars, drink beer, and screw frantically.

Patti thought I was at school, taking classes, working in the drama department, then stopping for a few drinks after work. Instead, I was in a drunken alternate universe where reality and drink-insanity intersected. There was no time or energy or willingness to think of right or wrong or consequences. If Patti fell for my lies, I figured it was her fault.

The game came to a quick end when Patti came to the campus one day to deliver some news and discovered I was no longer enrolled as a student. I had dropped out a couple of months earlier.

That night, she packed her bags and moved out. As far as I was concerned, it was good timing. I was ready to move Sherri in. But without Patti's salary to live on, I had to get a job — and the only job I could find was back at the Pavilion. Then Sherri's parents, disgusted by her decision to live with me, stopped paying their daughter's bills. So Sherri got work at another tourist attraction in the area, a dinner theater, where she waited on tables dressed in the shortest skirt I'd ever seen.

For a brief period, I made extra money working at the dinner theater myself, cast as one of the "boys" in *The Boys in the Band* and the lead in *Dr. Cook's Garden*. One night, much to my surprise, my parents, who had made it clear that they disapproved of everything I had done thus far with my life, came to see me. Sherri waited on their table and got a five-dollar tip from my old man who had no idea who she was.

The dinner theater closed when the owner stole the week's receipts and headed for parts unknown, screwing the director, the actors, and everybody else who had trusted him.

Sherri and I moved to a cheaper apartment and I started tending bar in a hippie joint on the beach. My drinking increased along with my opportunity to do it. The job was routine enough that I could do it drunk and pocket money without getting caught. Most nights, after the bar closed, I'd head to one of the nearby taverns. The bartenders who knew me, and that was most of them, never charged me. I, of course, returned the favor. That was the rule and it was a good rule as far as I was concerned.

One night, I came home to Sherri, unlocked the door, and heard the scurrying of a two-legged rat running through the kitchen and out the back. And that was pretty much the end of that relationship. I left Sherri or she left me, I'm not sure which, and I moved into an apartment above the garage of my older brother's house. By then, he was a dentist, married and with a couple of kids.

I was working as a bartender at The Tarheel Gaslamp Pub on Clearwater Beach. I got drunk every night without fail and never got home until just before sunrise, often with some woman who was lonely and goofy enough to be a bartender groupie.

One busy evening, a pretty brunette came up to the bar and stood there, looking at me expectantly. I walked over and asked her what she wanted to drink.

She smiled but said nothing.

"Listen, honey," I said. "You can't just stand here at the bar and not order a drink."

She stopped smiling. "You don't remember me, do you?"

Had I been sober, I would have said "Of course I remember you," and faked my way through the rest of the conversation. But I wasn't and I didn't.

"Have I seen you before?" I asked.

"You son-of-a-bitch," she said, her voice low and cold. "You son-of-a-bitch. I was with you last night. I fucked you last night."

She stormed out.

I vaguely remembered picking up someone and taking her to my garage apartment. "Jesus Christ," I thought. "She's beautiful. How the hell could I have forgotten her?"

I checked around and found out her name. Turns out she worked as a nurse at the local hospital. I called the hospital and asked for her. But before she could pick up the phone I hung up. "What the hell are you thinking?" I said to myself.

For a time after that, I seemed to be with a different woman every night, some young, some old, some pretty, some not so pretty. Most I don't remember. They were the women who were still sitting at my bar when it was time for last call, as lonely as I was, as desperate for company. As for the sex… that was just the ticket price we paid to be with somebody else.

Then Patti came back. We got into a serious conversation about how badly we had treated one another and decided to start over.

We rented an apartment and I went to work for her brother, as a carpenter, learning from the ground up. I still drank, but not while I was working. And I did some more acting, appearing in amateur productions of *Any Wednesday* and *The Mousetrap*. It looked like we had survived yet another marital collapse.

But after a year or so of fairly good behavior, I had a brief affair with an actress from the theater group. It wasn't my fault. She seduced me. Honest-to-God. But Patti didn't see it that way.

Kicked out of our apartment — and my job with Patti's brother — I once again went back to tending bar, this time at the VFW club in town. I rented a motel room and moved my few belongings in. I spent a drunken weekend with a woman from the VFW whose name I never learned. I stole not just money from the club but bottles of liquor, enough to stay drunk, to feed the demon nonstop. I learned how to pass out more than once in a day, managing to wake up, half sober, in time to go to work and start the cycle again.

My parents, who lived just a half-mile from me, let me know that I wasn't welcome in their home. I told them I didn't give a shit. I had another drink.

Patti and I got divorced a few months later and I moved into another garage apartment, just a few blocks from my favorite bar, the Horseshoe Tavern in downtown Clearwater.

The day the divorce was final, I went to the Horseshoe and put 20 dollars on the bar. I ordered 20 Snake Bites, a hooker of 7 Crown in a shot glass topped by a dollop of crème de menthe.

"Let me have all 20 at once," I said. "Just line them up."

The barman gave me a funny look but lined up 20 shot glasses and filled them. The other rummies in the bar glanced at the drinks, licked their lips, then looked away. I tossed them off, one after another. Then I echoed the last words of Dylan Thomas, one of my heroes: "I've had 20 straight whiskeys," I said. "I think that's the record." (Thomas had proclaimed his record — 18 straight whiskeys — just before he lapsed into a coma.)

That night I met my soon-to-be second wife, the eventual mother of my children. She walked into the VFW and stared drinking Budweiser from the can, my kind of gal.

WIFE TWO: MAKING BABIES

The Mother of My Children

Cathy was slim enough to be called skinny, with a bounce to her step, reddish-brown hair and freckles, and a smile that crinkled her eyes. She was also, though I didn't know it at the time, too young to be drinking.

For our first date, we went to the Pavilion for lunch and drank beer on the porch until the sun went down. The next day, I took her to my motel room where we spent the night. A few days later, we were living together. She was working, then, on the assembly line at an electronics firm in Largo, just south of Clearwater. I was tending bar at the VFW.

Drinking was at the center of my life and so, by extension, at the center of her life, too. She rarely got more than tipsy — still, our times together were constantly off-kilter, as if they'd been filmed with the camera tilted at a slight angle. I remember that she liked to touch the back of my hand when we were seated next to each other in a bar, but I don't remember her voice and I remember little of what we talked about.

One night, I got out of the motel bed we shared, drunk and naked, headed for the bathroom, and apparently became confused about where I was. With Cathy watching from the bed, I stood in the corner of the room, leaned forward against a wall, and pissed on the chair where she had left her clothes.

Years later, in the middle of one of our many arguments, she called me an alcoholic for the first time — and I couldn't believe my ears. I stared at her as if she were a crazy woman. "What the hell did you think you were marrying?" I shouted. "You didn't know what I was when I pissed on your jeans?"

In the beginning, though, there were no arguments. We moved from the motel room to a little bungalow where we set up something like housekeeping, with me drinking as much as I could and her tagging along, not exactly keeping up with me, but holding her own.

I soon lost my bartending job at the VFW and went to work as a janitor in a Jewish temple. I enjoyed the work but drank my way out of that job in a matter of weeks. A few days later, I learned that a chain of bars was looking for a janitorial service. I had no truck, no equipment, no business going after the contract, but I lied about all that in the interview. The next day, Cathy and I were the owner-operators of a cleaning service.

We took the back seat out of her car and used it to haul our cleaning equipment. After a few weeks, we had the money to buy a used van. Seven nights a week, beginning at 1:00 a.m., we were alone in one bar after another, doing what I considered to be light work for good money. And as a perk, I got to pour myself huge drinks all night long, one at each bar. I made sure not to pour from the same bottle two nights in a row, figuring the small thefts wouldn't be noticed by the bartenders. As soon as we came home, I'd pass out, waking in the afternoon to drink, then sleep, then work and drink all night. It was perfect.

It lasted about six months, and I don't believe I took a single sober breath that entire time. I floated on an alcoholic cloud at night and slept through alcoholic dreams during the day. I was insensate, which I took for happy.

In the midst of this madness, Cathy and I decided to have children together. In those days, that meant we had to get married. I bought a plastic wedding ring at a dime store and we got a marriage license. Cathy bought a dress long enough to hide her sandals. We made an appointment to be married by a justice of the peace at the local courthouse and made arrangements to have a reception at the VFW hall.

On the way to the courthouse, we stopped at the Horseshoe for a drink to settle our nerves. I started drinking screwdrivers and playing 9-ball for five dollars a game. I was shooting good pool that day. I felt like Minnesota Fats. Cathy finally managed to drag me out of the bar and drive us to the courthouse. I have no recollection of the ceremony.

Looking back, I have often wondered why none of the people I knew said anything about my drinking. Oh, comments were made, jokes at my expense, but no one ever tried to have a serious conversation about it with me. I never broached the subject either. In fact, I took great pains to avoid people who might have talked to me, warned me, taken some action… including my parents and my brothers.

Like most alcoholics, I surrounded myself with drinkers. It was easy to identify them. There's always a giveaway — the twitch, the averted glances, the strained laughter. Drunks seek out what the fellowship calls "lower companions" — those who seem to be in worse shape than they are. Lower companions won't call you on your bad behavior. Better still, their lives seem more miserable than yours. It's ironic, but a common characteristic of alcoholics is a sense of superiority. "I'm not that bad because he is worse." I've thought those words while standing at a bar with wet pants, unable to hold my head erect, slurring my words, unable to stop drinking.

Several months after we got married, Cathy was pregnant. I told myself I should stop drinking but I kept on. There were nights when I got so drunk I couldn't finish my part of the job. I'd forget to empty the trashcans or mop the floor or clean the toilets. Not surprisingly, we lost the contract. The official reason was "nonperformance" but I knew the truth. They had gotten wise to how much I was drinking.

Desperate for work, I sobered up for 12 hours and got a job as a garbage man in the city of Dunedin. I was happy to get it and it showed. On the second day, my supervisor complimented me. "Keep up the hard work," he said, "and someday we'll put you in charge of your own truck."

I threw my gloves on the ground and walked away. I might be a drunk, I remember thinking, but I'd be damned if I'd let this guy limit my future to driving a garbage truck.

We had no income and the little we had saved was running out. Desperate for work yet again, I got a job as an orderly in a nursing home. Cathy, so pregnant that she couldn't button her blouses, signed on as a nurse's aide. I'd drink beer in the morning and sneak out at lunchtime to grab a few more, stumble through the afternoon, and then drink at night, as much as the budget would allow. Pregnant, Cathy had to curtail her drinking, and that made me happy. More beer for me.

It was during that time that I went on my first drinking marathon. I started at a local tavern and when they closed, I went to an after-hours joint. When I ran out of money, I went to another bar and borrowed some. I continued like that, moving from bar to bar, borrowing money where I could, pawning my watch, running tabs in places where I was known. I had an old Pontiac station wagon that I'd bought for 50 dollars and I pretty much lived in that car for about a week, hoping the cops wouldn't notice me. I broke into my older brother's sailboat, berthed at a marina on Clearwater Beach, and slept a few nights on sail bags after turning the cabin upside down in search of booze or money or something to sell.

One morning, in a place called the Porpoise Pub, I was drinking a beer when I spotted a machine with hot dogs spinning slowly under a heater. I was instantly ravenous. I ordered one of the dogs, jammed it in my mouth, and took a big bite just as somebody slammed a door. I gasped and suddenly I couldn't breathe. I ran from one end of the bar to the other, clutching my throat and gesturing, hoping someone would figure out that I was choking. My eyes streaming, I ran out of the bar. Headed for I don't know where, I tripped over a concrete parking barrier and crashed to the asphalt, dislodging the chunk of hot dog.

"Shit," I thought, "I can't believe I almost died by strangling on a wienie in a bar."

That ended the marathon. I went home. Cathy was furious to the point of tears. She screamed at me. I cowered. Finally, I calmed her down by promising to go into treatment at the VA hospital in St. Petersburg.

I never had any intention of quitting. I told myself that I didn't have a real drinking problem — that there were plenty of drinkers who were in much worse shape. I could control my drinking. All I needed was a chance to clean myself up a bit.

I took time off from my job and stayed in the VA treatment program for four weeks — with my days spent in classes about alcoholism, listening to lectures, going to meetings of the AA fellowship, but mostly playing pool and watching television. The clearest memory I have of the lectures was being shown a slice of diseased human liver vacuum-packed in plastic. It was mildly effective. I wondered, for a moment, what my liver might look like. Then I thought, "To hell with it. That liver is from some old coot, not a young guy like me."

The only person who visited me while I was in treatment was a girl I worked with in the nursing home. Her name was Kathy (with a K). She and I had been mind-fucking each other for a couple of months. We'd meet in empty rooms and kiss and grope each other, and she'd flash me sometimes, spreading her long legs so I could see that she wasn't wearing panties under her white uniform. She was tall and skinny, with bad teeth and blonde hair. She had a body as tight as a trampoline.

Kathy and I went for a walk on the hospital grounds and stopped to do a little necking. Then we were screwing in the grass like a couple of dogs in heat. Afterward, rearranging our clothes, we heard cheering. We looked up and saw that a group of old guys had been standing on a balcony and watching us. They had a perfect line of sight. They were laughing and waving. And Kathy surprised me by waving back.

The Newshound

I stayed sober for a few months after that stint in treatment, hanging on by my fingernails, fighting the almost constant desire to drink — no, not to drink but to get rip-roaring drunk, to pour booze down my throat until my mind stopped running at top speed, until my hair stopped hurting, until my eyeballs stopped itching.

After work one day, I simply couldn't hang on any longer. I told myself that I'd have just a couple, just enough to take the edge off. I told Cathy I was going out on an errand and instead went to a bar where I ordered a draft beer. I gulped it down, barely swallowing, then another and another, drinking so fast that the beer ran down my chin and soaked my shirt. I kept drinking until, finally, I had no choice but to stumble home.

Cathy raged. She howled. She told me she was sick of me. But she didn't kick me out.

Soon after that, our son Dylan was born. Cathy's labor was long, too long for me to deal with. I left the hospital and went to an Irish bar where I bought one beer, bragged about being a new daddy, and then sat back and waited for the other rummies to buy me drinks in celebration. Some daddy! I made it back to the hospital just after the baby was born.

Standing with her father, who hated me, looking through the window into the room filled with newborns, he told the only joke I'd ever heard him tell. "He looks just like you," he said.

I felt proud. Then my father-in-law grinned. "Sure, he looks like you. Flat on his back with a bottle in his mouth."

I laughed, but I wanted to weep.

When Cathy and I brought Dylan home, I had to face facts. We couldn't even try to raise a child on the money I was making at the nursing home. I'd heard that an old schoolmate of mine, Terry Plumb, was now the managing editor of the local newspaper, the *Clearwater Sun*. Somehow I got the idea that I could be a newspaperman. After all, I'd been writing for years. Short stories. Poetry. Hell, I'd even written a couple of articles for the *Sun* when I was in Japan in the Air Force. I'd throw together a couple of "samples" and beg Terry for a job.

Terry and I met at a pub for lunch. I kept my drinking to a beer or two while we talked, though I was eyeing the booze bottles behind the bar. I told him that I'd just had a child and was in dire need of decent work. He came through. The paper would pay me 25 dollars a day for five days. If, in that time, I managed to write a story good enough for them to run, I'd be hired full-time.

I floated into the Horseshoe the next morning feeling like Hildy Johnson, the star reporter in the play *The Front Page*, looking forward to a job where I'd be able to hang out with my fellow newshounds at some colorful local tavern trading gossip about the pols, where my hard-bitten exterior and heart of gold would be appreciated. I wondered if I should buy a fedora and imagined myself accepting the Pulitzer for spot news.

For four and a half days, I followed every lead I could get my hands on, struggling to come up with something, anything, the paper could use. I went to a murder scene and got sick to my stomach looking at the corpse. I interviewed a female cop who was new to the local force and in writing it up I made every stylistic mistake known to journalism. I wrote three pages about a traffic accident only to have the copy editor cut it down to a single paragraph with no byline.

On my fifth and final day, a woman called the paper, looking to get some free publicity for herself, and I happened to take the call. She told me that she was riding a bicycle across Florida in an attempt to get enough signatures on a petition to have her name placed on the ballot for the next presidential election. When she told me she was a lesbian ex-nun, I got a tingle. The article wrote itself.

The next day, I reported to a news bureau in New Port Richey, about 15 miles north of Clearwater, to start my full-time job as a journalist. Somehow, I managed to hold on to that job for almost five years.

I was welcomed to the team by the bureau chief, a crack reporter named Oscar Brisky, with his version of a pep talk. "A newspaper is a copy-eating monster," he said. "Every day, you have to feed it by filling white space. That's your job and don't ever think otherwise."

Maybe he caught a whiff of my morning vodka or bourbon or whatever I'd guzzled that day because he followed that with something that might have been a warning: "The news business isn't like it is in the movies. Drunks don't make it. It's a profession and you have to act like a professional."

I did what I could to feed the copy-eating monster every day and I kept right on drinking, chewing mints and gum and gnawing on onions and keeping my hands in my pockets to hide my shakes.

I would start my day by drinking at home, a beer or a couple of shots to quiet my tremors. Then, on my way to the office, I would stop at a gin mill, the Tennessee Tavern or a place on Highway 19 where they made killer vodka martinis for breakfast. It wasn't unusual for me to have three or four mixed drinks before I got to work. I'd check the overnight police and fire reports over the phone. Then it was off to the county courthouse to see what I could stir up there. By that time, it was mid-morning and the shakes were coming back, so I'd stop in a bar for a couple of drinks, then back to the office to write and gather news for the next day's edition.

I covered crime and politics, often intermingled, and I felt like a huge fish in a very tiny pond. I was known around town. The local politicians treated me like I was important. I made enough money to drink as much as I wanted so long as I stayed away from top-shelf booze. When I got in trouble, I talked my way out of it.

I learned how to make myself vomit so I could pour more liquor in my gut, swishing water in my yap so I wouldn't breathe puke breath on whatever lonely woman I was trying to pick up or impress. One night, I picked up a hairdresser and took her to a cheap hotel. She had an epileptic seizure while we were screwing and, for a second or two, I thought she was being driven mad by her desire for me. I left her trembling on the bed, hoping she wouldn't die. I missed a deadline after I passed out in the bathroom of the newsroom and I blamed it on the janitor who, I said, must have inadvertently thrown my deathless prose in the trash. I mistakenly identified the State's Attorney as the suspect in a rape case.

But despite my drunkenness, I wrote some good articles. And thanks to Oscar Brisky, who was a real newsman, I learned to write fast and clean.

The Bottom Falls Out

Cathy and I were not getting along. We hardly talked. We never made love. Truth be told, we didn't much like each other. And there were good reasons. My drinking was hindering our ability to keep up with the bills. We were forced to move into a raggedy trailer about 10 miles north of New Port Richey. It was barely large enough for two people. Dylan slept in a crib in our tiny bedroom.

But the situation had a silver lining for me. The trailer was on a remote piece of property owned by a redneck who ran an illegal all-night bar out of his house. And I could get a drink whenever I wanted, usually for free or on the cheap.

Fourth of July weekend, I decided to go to a festival in a nearby small town, figuring I might be able to get a story out of it. I spotted Linda, a reporter for a local weekly, in the crowd. She was snapping pictures. I had met her at a press conference and saw her a few times at city council meetings. She was tall and slender, with short black hair and a mannish way about her. I'd never paid much attention to her but on that day I was ready for a fling.

As the festivities were winding down, she walked over to where I was standing.

"Hey," she said. "Glad this is done."

I nodded.

"How about a beer?" she said. "My treat."

Ten minutes later we were in a booth in a waterfront bar called Shrimper's Paradise with a pitcher of beer on the table between us. It had been about four hours since my last drink, so my hand trembled when I picked up the pitcher to pour. That was okay, though, a drink or two and I'd be steady as a rock. I filled two glasses. Linda's hand shook a bit when she picked up hers.

"God, that's good," she said after taking a deep drink and licking a little foam mustache from her upper lip. I nodded. As we finished that first pitcher of beer, we made plans. She'd stay at the bar. I'd run back to my office and write a quick article about the festival for the next day's paper. I'd be back in an hour, an hour-and-a-half at the most.

By the time the sun was fully set, I was back in the booth with Linda. We knocked off another pitcher of beer together, then drove to a bar where we could get some real booze. After that, we went to her place and screwed.

I didn't go home that night. The next day, while I was sleeping, Linda went shopping and bought some clothes for me. She told me she wanted me to stay. So I did. I put Cathy and Dylan out of my mind. I refused to face the fact that I'd left them stuck in a little trailer in the middle of nowhere, with no car and no money and about a four-mile walk to civilization.

After three or four days, though, it was hard to ignore what I had done. I decided to go home again. It wouldn't be the first time I'd come crawling back. Fuck her if she couldn't take a joke.

So I drove out to the little trailer, expecting to find a pissed-off wife that I'd be able to placate. Soon enough, everything would be back to normal, or at least back to what passed for normal in my life. But when I got to the trailer, Cathy and Dylan were gone. The trailer was empty except for a beer bottle that lay on its side in the middle of the sagging living room floor and a bunch of fat flies that buzzed around the kitchen sink. My clothes and all my records — old Bob Dylan and Joan Baez and Lead Belly albums that I'd had for years — had been tossed out in the yard, ruined.

"Fuck it," I said. It was the only thing I could think to say. Then I drove back to Linda's and had a drink.

It didn't take long for me to grow tired of Linda. I suppose I blamed her for losing my son. Whatever had been appealing about her was gone. I noticed the stained housecoat she wore day after day and the hair, a single hair, that grew on the bridge of her nose. She chewed with her mouth open, she walked funny, and when she was angry, she said things like "poopy."

We fought. We made up. I threatened to leave her and she threatened to kill herself. I went to a bar to drink and she called the police to report me for abuse. Finally, I had enough. While she was in the shower, I stole five checks from her purse. I got drunk that night and cashed them — two for 10 dollars, three for 5 dollars, and one for 3 dollars. I did a pretty good job of forging her signature but, master criminal that I was, I made the checks out to myself and used my press card as identification. I figured if the checks were for less than 50 bucks, the forgeries would be misdemeanors. I was wrong.

I called Cathy's parents and, as I suspected, she and Dylan were staying with them. Turning on my alcoholic charm, I begged her to give me another chance, to work with me on rebuilding our marriage. I truly did love Cathy, at least in my own sick way, and I certainly loved my son and missed him.

I talked her into spending the night with me in a motel in Clearwater. I promised to lighten up on the drinking, to stop entirely if she'd come back to me, and she did.

We rented a two-bedroom apartment in New Port Richey. I painted the smaller bedroom baby blue and filled it with stuffed rabbits and bears and a Mickey Mouse doll that was bigger than Dylan. For a time, I stopped drinking. It wasn't easy, but I did it.

I shook for the first few days and then I started to feel pretty good. I ate better, Cathy and I got along better, and we even started talking about having another kid. I wasn't happy though. I felt jumpy, unnerved.

When I looked at other people, they looked to me as if they were perfectly content, as if they paid all their bills on time, had good marriages, and looked forward to going to work every day. I wanted desperately to feel the way they looked… and I knew how to do it. All it would take was one beer. Just one.

On my way to a city council meeting, I turned my car into the parking lot of a beer joint I'd never been in and ordered a draft.

I was off and running. Within days, it was as if I'd never stopped drinking. Once again, I was stopping off on the way to work for vodka martinis on the rocks. I'd leave the office after a few hours to check out what was happening at the county courthouse and stop on the way for screwdrivers. I'd be so drunk by lunchtime that I'd have to go home and sleep for a few hours. Then I'd go back to the office, again stopping off to drink on the way.

I took to sleeping in the family room, and Cathy didn't mind. At our best, we could sit at dinner and make believe we were a normal family, but the effort of maintaining the illusion was taking its toll.

Then, early one morning when I was sitting at my desk, a sheriff's car wheeled into the parking lot and came to a stop. A deputy I didn't know strode into the office.

"You Doherty?" he asked.

"Yes," I answered. "What's up?"

"You're under arrest," he said, reaching for the handcuffs on his belt. "Five counts of forgery. Five counts of receiving goods in exchange for a forged instrument."

The deputy hustled me into the back of his car. Within an hour, I was being arraigned before a judge I happened to know.

"Well, Mr. Doherty," the judge said, "what have we here? I'm more used to seeing you in one of the press seats."

He looked at the paper in front of him. "Hmmm. Five counts of forgery. Really 10 counts."

"Holy shit," I thought. I'd covered dozens of cases in the judge's court, I'd hobnobbed with him at several social events, I liked him. I think he liked me, too. But business was business.

He looked over the tops of his half-glasses. "Bail is set at $8,500."

I don't know what possessed me. Maybe I was still half-drunk. I looked at the judge.

"Will you take a check, your honor?" I said.

He didn't laugh.

Oscar Brisky lent me the money to post bail. Amazingly, he didn't fire me. Also amazing… Cathy took me back again. But this time, we both agreed, I'd have to quit drinking for real. This was my last chance.

It didn't take long for the wheels of justice to turn. Within a couple of months, I'd pled guilty and been placed on probation for 10 years with the stipulation that I avoid alcohol completely and that I take Antabuse, a drug that would make me feel deathly ill if I took even one drink.

The arrest and conviction threw me a scare. For more than a year, I lived up to the terms of my probation. Every few days, I'd go to my probation officer's office to get one of my pills and I'd pop it into my mouth right in front of him. And in that period of enforced sobriety, Cathy and I got along. I was writing well, producing a lot of copy. I even got a raise. We saved money, enough to be able to buy an older tract home on a big piece of land outside New Port Richey. Things were good, so good that Cathy and I decided to have another child.

My life was ordered. I was paying bills on time. I was going to be a father and I was getting along with my wife. I should have been happy. But it seemed that something was missing, something without which I was incomplete.

Once again, I became obsessed with the idea of having a drink — you know, just one to take the edge off. I was working hard, not screwing around, I deserved it, right?

I've heard insanity described as doing the same thing over and over and expecting different results. That works for me because I once again found myself believing that I could take one drink, maybe two, and stop. Believing, despite all the evidence to the contrary, that I could drink the way I wanted to drink, like a gentleman, like James Bond sauntering up to the bar in a casino and ordering a martini, shaken not stirred. Never mind that I'd never sauntered in my life and that once I poured a drink down my gullet, I'd willingly drink panther piss if somebody told me it would get me drunk.

There was also the problem of the Antabuse — but I figured out a way to work around it. I'd go to my P.O.'s office, get my pill, and, as usual, pop it into my yap in front of him. But then I'd slide it over to the side, between my teeth and my cheek, and then spit it out on the way to my car. I thought I was the smartest guy ever born.

For a while, I drank slowly, only a few at a time. I'd even quit for a week or two and then start again. Then one morning, early, I left the house to drive to Dade City, about 40 miles away, to cover some tiresome public meeting that nobody really cared about. As I pulled out of the driveway, I had no intention of doing anything other than my job. Go to the meeting, take some notes, snap a couple of pics, come back to the office, write a story, try to find something else to fill some white space, go home, watch television, closing my eyes every time someone on screen looked like they were having a good time with a glass in their hand, and go to bed.

As I drove, I composed the lead paragraph of the story I expected to write, following the journalistic formula of putting the important crap first — the who, what, where, when, why.

I swung off Highway 19 and headed east on State Road 52. On the left, as I crested a small rise, stood a beer-and-wine joint I'd passed hundreds of times, never stopping. But this time, as soon as I saw the sign, I felt an urgent need for a beer. It was stronger than the need for release by a person on the verge of an orgasm, stronger than the need for food by a starving man. It could only be compared, I think, to the need for air by a person who was suffocating.

"What the hell," I thought. I put the car into a skid getting into the parking lot.

Drunken Son-of-a-Bitch

I never did get to the meeting in Dade City. Instead I drove to Tampa, where I rented a motel room. I drank and I didn't eat. The big story in the news was that a serial killer was attacking prostitutes and dumping their bodies in orange groves in Pasco County. I'd been to several of the dump-sites, had taken a picture of a skull flashing its terrible teeth under eyes filled with maggots. In my drunkenness, I decided to catch the killer. My plan was to hit all the bars on the strip and ask all the right questions.

I hit all the bars — but instead of asking questions, all I did was drink. Days passed by in brief flashes of consciousness, scenes from a mad movie cut and spliced into incomprehensibility. I visited an old girlfriend at a store in a shopping mall not far from my motel. I figured she'd be glad to see me. But she called mall security and they sent me packing.

Leaving the mall, I headed down a four-lane highway, going the wrong way. I realized my mistake when a car screamed past me, brights flashing wildly. I jerked the wheel. My car, a little Mazda about as long as a shoebox, slammed across the grassy median. I came to a rest headed in the right direction and undamaged. All seemed well until I realized I'd wet myself.

To comfort myself I tried to hire the services of a hooker. She was young and skinny with a gray cast to her skin that made me shudder. Her eyes darted wildly as if she were being hunted. I had the notion that she was diseased but I didn't care.

"You're fucked up, man," she said, shaking her head. "And you smell bad."

I offered her more money.

"You couldn't buy a woman if you were the warden in a women's prison with a bagful of pardons," she said, laughing.

I wondered how long she'd been waiting for a chance to use that line.

After three or four days, I drove back to New Port Richey. It was mid-morning when I stopped at a bar on the highway just a mile or so from the newspaper office. I was sick, shaky, unready and unwilling to go home where I knew Cathy would be waiting and angry. I staggered into the bar and ordered a drink in a take-out cup. I drove to the office, parked the car, and sat there drinking it, hoping it would make me feel a little better. Finally, I tilted the seat back, closed my eyes, and fell asleep.

The sound of someone pounding on the top of the car jerked me awake. My mouth was furry. I stared out the driver's side window. It was Oscar Brisky, my boss, leaning down to look at me, mouthing words I couldn't hear as he signaled for me to lower the window.

"Go home," he said. "Go home and come back when you sober up."

Without another word, he turned and walked into the building.

When I got home, things were as bad as might be expected. Cathy, hugely pregnant, cried when I walked in the door. "You tell me you love me," she said. "I believe you and then you do this to me. You build a house of cards and then tear it apart. You bastard!"

I wanted to reach out to her but I couldn't make my hands move. I knew I deserved her anger. Dylan was only 2 years old but he knew something was wrong between Cathy and me. He tried to please his mother by ignoring me or running away when I tried to hold him or talk to him.

When I went to the office the next day, Oscar told me the paper's managing editor — a new guy, not my old friend — wanted to see me. The ME was in Clearwater, about 30 miles away.

"I'll drive," said Oscar, picking up his keys.

We made the trip in silence, then entered the busy newsroom, filled with desks and noise. Oscar took a seat at one of the desks and gestured for me to go to the back of the room to the ME's glassed-in office. As I walked past the other reporters, men and women I'd known for a couple of years, they turned away.

The managing editor wasted no time. He told me he was sorry but that the newspaper couldn't afford to keep a loose cannon like me on the payroll. He told me I'd be given a week's severance but that my days as a reporter for the *Clearwater Sun* were over.

"Well," I said to Oscar, "that's that."

He nodded. "I went to bat for you," he said, "but it didn't help. I tried to get him to give you another chance but his mind was made up."

After that, I forced myself not to drink. I white-knuckled it, hanging on by dint of sheer willpower. I managed to talk myself into a job as an editor with the throwaway weekly newspaper in town, making roughly half what I'd been making at the *Sun*, but at least I was working. My boss, the publisher, was a nice guy but my duties were onerous. In addition to rewriting press releases and copy submitted by mostly no-talent stringers, I had to come up with a dozen or more of my own articles every week, attend functions as a representative of the publication, take and develop photos, lay out the paper, and help with paste-up.

Still, it was a newspaper — and I enjoyed the sense of being a big fish in an admittedly small pond. I felt as if I were at the center of the action in town, in a position to know the wheelers and dealers. From time to time, I could even make myself believe I was a real journalist. That I counted for something.

At home, as Cathy's due date got closer and closer, it seemed that things between the two of us were settling down. I'd come home from work and spend time with Dylan before dinner. We'd sit down together, I'd say grace, and we would eat and talk and, for the most part, say the right things. Cathy and I were sleeping in the same bed again and we were affectionate, loving even. But we were both aware, without ever saying a word, that the apparent normalcy of our relationship could be swept away in the time it took for me to down one drink.

When Cathy started to go into labor, my in-laws came to pick up Dylan and take him back to their house. Then I drove Cathy to the hospital and, like a dutiful husband, sat in the waiting room until our second child — a baby boy we named Eamon — was born. Once Cathy was settled in her room, I was allowed to see her. She was tired after the birth, looking wan and drawn as she smiled down at the baby in her arms. Standing next to her bed, I felt like we were a normal, happy family. Grinning, I kissed Cathy's cheek and told her I'd see her in the morning.

Driving home, I had to pass the Dew Drop Inn, one of my old hangouts. Without thinking, I wheeled into the parking lot. As soon as I walked into the bar and breathed the heady odor of stale beer, stale cigarette smoke, and misery, I felt at home.

I ordered a glass of Mad Dog and a beer back up. I lifted the glass of cheap wine to my lips and tossed it off. The thick liquid made me gag, slightly, but then I felt that wonderful icy punch right at the base of my skull, the same icy punch I'd felt the first time I drank and the second time and every time after that.

I don't remember leaving the bar, don't remember going home, all I remember is waking up the next morning, needing a drink, desperate for a drink. I drove to the Tennessee Tavern, another one of my old hangouts, and sat down at the bar. The barmaid nodded at me as if she'd seen me the day before.

"The usual, Hon?" she asked.

It was the alcoholic's greeting in every bar in the world. The usual? Get ready to die.

I nodded and put a couple of bucks on the bar. That quickly, that easily, I was on the treadmill again.

The experts say alcoholism is a progressive disease — that the disease gets worse even when the alky isn't drinking and that an alcoholic who picks up after a period of sobriety will start drinking as if there had been no interruption. It's true. For the next year, I drank as if I'd never stopped. Cathy came home from the hospital with the new baby and I was drunk. The baby cried in the middle of the night and, drunk, I picked him up out of his crib and trudged in circles, until, finally, I couldn't stand the crying anymore and I smacked his back.

"Did you hit the baby?" Cathy called out from our bed.

"I burped him," I snarled, and she jumped up and took him out of my arms.

I went to work drunk, so drunk that I could barely find my desk, so drunk that when I did find my desk, I'd lock my office door and go to sleep with my head on the typewriter. The shakes were so bad that I had to drink in the morning or run the risk of going into a seizure or having *delirium tremens*, the hallucinations and uncontrollable tremors that afflict chronic, late-stage rummies.

Before I went to bed I'd put a rocks glass on the counter next to the kitchen sink, fill the glass so full of booze that it almost spilled over, then stick a straw into it. When I woke up, I'd stumble to the sink and bend over so I could sip from the glass without trying to lift it to my lips. I'd puke in the sink, then lower my head to take another sip, hoping it would hit me fast. Then I'd pick up the glass and toss it off.

On weekends, while Cathy was still sleeping, I'd take a drink or a half-pint to the living room, sit on the sofa, and try to write editorials on a typewriter I had set up on the coffee table.

Dylan would often creep from his bed to join me. He'd ask me to get him some chocolate milk and he would kneel on the floor next to the sofa, leaning over a little toy typewriter I had bought for him. I'd type a few lines and take a drink. He'd look at me, type a few lines, then take a drink of chocolate milk. I thought it was great.

Every once in a while, I would slow down my drinking — and almost instantly things would seem almost normal. During one of those rare semi-sober periods, not long after Eamon's birth, I was invited to a press party at Busch Gardens in Tampa. In those days, Anheuser-Busch had a brewery on the grounds of the park, and visitors were treated to free beer. Though I was trying to keep myself under control, the idea was appealing. Cathy and I packed up the car with the kids and all their paraphernalia and drove the 30 miles to Tampa as if we were an ordinary family out for an outing. The only signs that we weren't all that normal were the tall can of beer I held between my thighs as I drove and the lack of any communication worth a damn.

As we neared the park, we passed a rundown, one-story building that once may have been a neighborhood grocery store. According to a sign in the grime-streaked window, it was now a walk-in plasma center, a place where the unemployed and homeless could have their blood drawn, wait for several hours as the plasma was separated from it, and then have their plasma-less blood cells pumped back into their bodies. All for the princely sum of 15 bucks.

Business was booming that day. A line stretched from the front door around the corner. Men and a few women lounged against the window, smoking, dirty, and unkempt.

"Daddy, who are those people?" Dylan asked.

"They're poor people who have to sell their blood for money to eat," I said.

"To drink," Cathy said. "Not to eat, to drink."

I didn't answer. Dylan, apparently satisfied, went back to his coloring book. I took a swallow of beer.

"Keep going and that's where you'll end up," Cathy said to me.

"What? What are you talking about now?"

"Big deal newspaper editor," she sniffed. "Just keep drinking and you'll be standing in that line someday, wondering what the hell hit you."

"You're nuts," I said.

On my 33rd birthday, instead of going to work, I spent the day in a bar. Then I went home. But I felt constrained at home, jumpy, anxious to get out again, to get away, to lose myself. I told Cathy I had work to do at the office and I left her standing in the living room, cursing my back. I returned to the bar. The barmaid grinned when I walked back in and set a shot of tequila and a beer wash on the counter. I drank. I don't know how much but enough that when I got up to leave the barmaid insisted on taking my keys.

"No way," I said. "I ain't givin' up my keys.

"You gotta let me call you a cab, Sweetie," she said.

We argued, but nicely, and finally I agreed to take a cab home, provided I could keep my keys so I could pick up my car in the morning. She laughed, shook her head sadly, and called a cab. In a few minutes, it pulled up outside and I hopped in.

"Where to, buddy?"

I managed to pull a five-spot from my pocket and hand it to him.

"Here," I said. "Just take me to the back lot so I can get my car."

Without a word, the cabby grabbed the bill and drove around the building to where my car was parked.

The next thing I knew, I was coming out of a blackout — that strange state when an alky acts as if he's conscious while the higher centers of his brain are unplugged, off-circuit — just as my car left the road about 100 yards from my home. I think I screamed when I realized I was heading toward a small billboard. I know I screamed when the car punched through the billboard, then knocked over a small orange tree, ripped half the side porch off a frame house, rammed into another small tree, and came to rest against a fence.

My face felt wet and blood poured down the front of my shirt. I lifted my hand to my nose and felt pain. The steering wheel was cracked. Suddenly a man in a robe, the owner of the house, was there, helping me out of the car.

"Oh, my God," he yelped, "are you okay? What can I do for you?"

I staggered and leaned against the car. "You can get me a drink," I said. "You can get me a fuckin' drink."

Maybe 15 minutes later, after the police cars arrived and I was standing handcuffed with some gauze stuffed up my nostrils, washed by the flashing red and blue lights, I looked up and saw Cathy about six feet away. She'd heard the sirens and walked down the street to investigate. The baby was in her arms. Dylan was at her side, his eyes wide, his thumb stuck in his mouth.

"Look at your father," Cathy said. "Look at your father, the drunken son-of-a-bitch. Look at him because you'll never see him again."

Weaving back and forth, looking at my sons, the boys I claimed to love, the only thought in my head was, "Good. Get the little bastards out of here. Get 'em out of here and just let me drink."

No Recourse

There are few things in life as miserable as a drunkard's heebie-jeebies and few places worse to have them than a Florida sheriff's holding tank. By the time I was hauled away from the spot where I'd driven my car into a house, was booked, and was pushed into the tiny cell stinking of urine and sweat, I was already in the full grip of early alcohol withdrawal.

My guts writhed with the need for a drink, my hands shook when I tried to scratch my scalp, loud noises made me jump, my breath, foul as a buzzard's, came in short gasps. I knew, from the few times I'd tried to go cold turkey on my own, that it wouldn't take long before I'd do just about anything for a drink.

But it never got to that. The sheriff's department screwed up. Driving drunk was a direct violation of my probation. They should have notified the court. Had they done so, I would have been sentenced to jail. Period. Instead, I was allowed to post bail and walk. I couldn't believe it. I skulked out of the courtroom with a smirk on my face. I was ready to drink some more.

But first, I had to slink home and plead with Cathy to let me in the house.

"Look," I said to her, "I'm going to be locked up soon enough. We both know that. So why not let me stay here a little longer — just till I fuck up. Then I'll be out of your hair for good."

It worked.

The first thing I did when I got back in the house was locate a bottle of booze I'd hidden in the laundry room and toss off enough to steady my shaking hands. I worried that someone in the sheriff's office would realize the mistake they had made and come for me. But after a few days, I started to relax. Maybe I had slipped through the cracks. I talked some desperate used car salesman into selling me an old clunker of a VW and went back to work at the weekly, with the understanding, spelled out by the publisher, that it was a temporary arrangement.

Needless to say, I kept drinking. Mad Dog and beer, an occasional shot of booze in one of the gin mills in town, a half-gallon of wine in the laundry room, a fifth of crap buried in the backyard. It was enough to take care of my immediate needs, but I wasn't dumb enough to believe that I could stave off trouble for very long. I planned an escape to Mexico, tantalized by the freedom I imagined I'd have there. But I didn't do more than plan. I simply didn't have the energy.

I slept in the den, tilted back in my old recliner. I slept drunk and woke up drooling. I slept the sleep of a drunk with my mouth wide open. I was terrified that palmetto bugs, big as hummingbirds, would fly into my open maw and make a home for themselves there while I slept. To protect myself, I kept a tennis racquet by the side of the chair so I could slap away at the bugs as they attacked — or as I imagined they attacked. I heard voices that I knew weren't voices. I saw ghosts moving in the room while I watched TV.

I knew I was low, very low. "I've got to quit," I'd tell myself. "Tomorrow. I'll do it tomorrow."

I meant it. From the bottom of my heart I meant it. But when you're a drinking alcoholic, it makes no difference if you want to quit. You must drink. That's what being an alcoholic is.

I would go for days without bathing. I stunk from the Mad Dog and the armpits of my shirts were stained red with sweat from my body's futile effort to flush the cheap, fortified wine out of my system.

Once, reeking, I tried to crawl into bed with Cathy.

"Get out of here," Cathy said. "If you touch me, I'll throw up."

I was ashamed and I took that to be a good thing. I was still human enough to feel shame. It gave me a temporary lift. And so I went back to the living room and congratulated myself with a drink.

The call I'd been dreading came while I was sitting at my desk in my office. It was from a lieutenant in the sheriff's department that I'd used as a source, a nice guy.

"I just wanted to give you a heads-up," he said. "We're going to arrest you tomorrow."

I thought for a moment. It was Tuesday.

"How about I turn myself in Thursday morning?" I said. "That'll give me a chance to put the paper to bed one more time."

I don't know why I expected him to care — or why it mattered to me. Maybe I figured that if I could get the paper out one more time, I might garner some credit for myself somewhere.

"I should be able to make that happen," he said. "But make sure you really do turn yourself in on Thursday or we're both screwed."

I put the paper out, somehow, working around the hours I spent swilling wine and beer. Meanwhile, Cathy had no idea what was going on. For some reason — fear, perhaps, or maybe shame, or maybe I just didn't give a damn — I simply could not tell her I was going to prison.

Thursday morning, I went into the bedroom where Dylan was sleeping and Eamon was twitching and cooing in his crib. I kissed the top of the baby's head and knelt down and hugged Dylan. He stirred and looked at me curiously. I said goodbye, told him I loved him, and left.

Of course, I couldn't go straight to the sheriff's office. I had to prime myself first. I walked the mile or so from the house to a bar that I knew would be open that early. Except for the barmaid, it was empty. I took a seat and ordered vodka on the rocks. I was trembling. I lifted the drink to my lips and grimaced. But as soon as the booze hit my gut, I felt better. My shakes eased enough so I could light a smoke. All I needed was a few more shots and I'd be okay, I'd be ready to turn myself in.

The barmaid put my second drink on the bar and I tossed it off, nodding. I drank until my money ran out. Then I told her I was going to prison and she bought me a drink. Just as I finished that, a couple of construction workers came in and she told them my story. They bought me another drink, clapping me on the back and telling me everything would be okay. When it was clear that no more free drinks would be coming my way, I left the joint with my head down, good and drunk.

I made my way to the sheriff s office, weaving, my eyes squinting against the white brightness of the mid-morning sun. In the parking lot, I tripped on a concrete barrier and fell to the ground, scraping my hands on the gravel surface. A deputy I didn't know ran over to help. He knelt at my side.

"Jesus," he muttered, "you're as drunk as a coot."

"I'm here to see the sheriff," I mumbled. "I got to turn myself in."

The deputy helped me to my feet and guided me into the building. Within minutes, I was in the holding tank, my shoelaces and belt gone, curled on a thin mattress on a metal platform, my head spinning.

"Well," I thought, "this is it."

Bye Bye, Baby, Bye Bye

I passed out and stayed out for a while. When I came to, I was in need of a drink, desperate need — and the need didn't go away.

It took a while for the powers that be to decide how to handle my case. They finally shifted me from New Port Richey to the main county jail in Dade City.

In the meantime, I forced myself to drink the warm milk and chicory coffee they brought me at mealtimes, to take little bites of the bologna sandwiches and lumpy grits and powdered eggs. I knew, from experience, what would happen if I didn't. Years earlier, when I was married to Patti, I'd had a seizure when I tried to stop drinking too quickly — and I was terrified, as I sat alone in the small cell, that I'd have another one and die before anybody found me.

After about three days, I was handcuffed and put in a van with a couple of other prisoners for transport to Dade City. As I sat in the van, a deputy knocked on the window. I scrunched around so I could reach the window crank with my handcuffed hands. I lowered the window.

"There's somebody here to talk to you," he said.

Cathy walked up to the van, holding out a quit claim deed to our house.

"If you sign this, maybe I can sell the house and the kids and I can survive," she said tersely.

I couldn't look her in the eyes. I nodded. She handed me a ballpoint pen and I clumsily managed to scribble my signature. I handed the paper back, feeling sick, feeling the other men in the van staring at me.

"Goodbye," she said.

She turned and walked away.

"Fuck you," I thought. "I'll be okay."

One More Break

By rights, I should have gone to prison. That's what I expected to happen. Instead, I was held in the Dade City Jail for almost six months and then dragged back before the judge who had originally sentenced me.

During those six months, I sat in a cell in an old, crowded, two-story relic of a building, trying to figure out what I could do, if anything, to salvage the train wreck that my life had become. I kept thinking that if only Cathy and I could get back together so I'd have Dylan and Eamon in my life, I'd have the impetus I needed to control my drinking. I'd get some kind of job to make money while I got serious about my writing, and we'd all be fine. We could put this behind us.

I never gave any serious thought to cutting out the booze entirely. To my mind, if things were going my way, I'd be able to drink like all those other people who could have one or two and then stop. It didn't occur to me that whenever I started drinking, even when I intended to say, "No thanks, I think I've had enough!" after one or two, I never could get myself to say those words. Instead, I'd slide my glass forward and nod.

"Sure, pal," I'd say. "Hit me again."

The Japanese have a proverb: "First the man takes a drink, then the drink takes a drink, then the drink takes the man." The drink was taking me. I just couldn't or wouldn't admit it.

The food in the county lockup was abysmal. Slightly underweight to begin with, I lost 30 pounds. The cells, tiny little warrens with eight bunks and an open toilet, were crowded. In most of them, at least one man slept on the floor. Men slept on tables in the day room and in shower stalls. There was no such thing as exercise unless you count fights. Many men, including me, saw the sky only on brief trips out of the jail for court hearings. And most of those being held had not yet been found guilty of a crime.

I decided to write an article about the jail — not because of any journalistic drive to expose the crowded, unsanitary conditions, the lack of decent food, the noise, but because I figured I might be able to make a few bucks with it.

I mailed the article to Oscar Brisky. He paid me 25 dollars and published it.

It got noticed. As a result, the county judge who'd sentenced me reviewed every inmate's file. Then he toured the jail. He found that most of the men were awaiting trial on nonviolent charges, and he ordered most of them released without bail. Since I was being held on a probation violation, I was not one of those set free.

When I was finally taken to court for sentencing, I was expecting to be sent to prison. Instead, the judge — the same one — placed me back on probation with a requirement that I go into the alcohol treatment program being run by the Salvation Army in Tampa.

"If I see you here again," he said, "bring your toothbrush."

EVEN THE SALVATION ARMY GIVES UP ON ME

Gotta Quit!

There are worse places to be than the Salvation Army residence in downtown Tampa. The alcohol treatment center and living quarters were on the top floor of a large old building filled with offices and dormitories for the Salvation Army's soldiers. The ground floor housed a chapel, a dining hall, a resale shop, and a huge warehouse.

Sally, as we alkies refer to the Salvation Army, took me to her breast as soon as I walked in the door. I was welcomed, shuffled to an office where I filled out some papers, shown to a room, and told I'd start the 28-day treatment the next day. It wasn't home, but, hey, it beat the hell out of a jail cell.

That first night, while watching television in the rec room with the other rummies, one of the guidance counselors walked in and told me there was someone in the lobby downstairs who wanted to see me.

The rec room, by the way, was a former storage space that had been fitted out with a couple of grungy sofas that they couldn't sell in the Sally store, and the television was an old, cranky, black-and-white set with rabbit ears.

As I took the elevator to the first floor, I wondered who on earth could be visiting me. I hadn't been in touch with anybody since being put back on probation and ordered into treatment. I'd been taken from the courtroom back to jail where I spent three or four more nights sleeping on the steel bunk before being hauled from Dade City down to Tampa. Could Cathy have decided to give me another shot? I'd called my old man to let him know what was going on but he'd hung up on me. Could he have had a change of heart? Could it be one of my brothers? I didn't really expect any of them to want to see me... but maybe, I thought.

When I got to the lobby, the only person there was the uniformed Salvation Army warrior behind the desk.

"What's up?" I asked.

"Are you Kieran Doherty?"

I nodded. He held a thick envelope in my direction.

"I thought someone wanted to see me," I said, trying not to sound as down as I suddenly felt.

"Sorry," the warrior said. "Just me. Somebody dropped this off for you."

I opened the envelope as I rode the elevator back upstairs. Inside was a sheaf of papers informing me that Cathy was filing for divorce… and that her intention, the intention of her lawyer (who had been provided by the state), was that I not be allowed any unsupervised visits with my sons… and that before each supervised visit, I'd have to go to the sheriff's office to be tested for drugs and alcohol.

"Shit," I thought. I wasn't surprised. Still, I wondered, "Was I really that bad?" I knew the answer was yes.

Part of my treatment involved group therapy led by a longhaired, gentle woman named Doris. Doris's world was all about incense and feelings and Seals & Crofts and hugs, lots of hugs. I didn't mind hugging Doris. She had a nice, tight little body and wasn't afraid to show it off along with her peace and love and serenity.

During my first session, we hugged and sat on pillows on the floor listening to "Summer Breeze." Then Doris passed out pieces of paper and pencils.

"I'd like each of you to write something good about yourself," she said. "One thing that makes you proud and happy to be you. Then we'll read out what we wrote and share our feelings."

I'd never in my life given any thought to what was good about me. Around me, the other dozen or so drunks in the group chattered away and giggled kind of nervously before bending over their papers to write.

I sat still. I tried to think of something good about myself. "I'm a good person," I tried. No, that's not really true. "I'm a good lover?" Nope. "Husband?" Hell no. "Worker?" Can't really say that, can I? "Son… Catholic… writer?" Nothing. I couldn't come up with anything I could feel good about. Then I thought, "Well, I'm a good father. I love my boys." For a moment, I was suffused with joy. Finally, there was something good I could say about myself. "I love Dylan and Eamon!" And I did. I knew I did!

But then reality set in. How the hell could I say that? What kind of father had I been? Yes, I loved them, but I never loved them the way a father should. I'd cheated myself out of that, hadn't I? And I was surprised, stunned, by the sudden sadness I felt. I started weeping and I wept as if I'd never stop, until my chest and belly hurt and my throat was sore.

"I've gotta quit!" I thought. "I've gotta quit!"

I finished the program at the Salvation Army and then volunteered to go through it again, just to be safe. I really did want to stop drinking. I was starting to like the fellowship meetings I was going to, even though the people there seemed to look down on me because I was so young. At 30-something, I was a kid to them. Some even called me "kid."

With my second 28-day stint coming to an end, I begged my brothers to help me out so I could buy a car and look for a job and they came through with 150 dollars. I found an old, old Dodge for 140 dollars, and bought it with the understanding that I'd pick it up the day I got out of treatment. I used one of Sally's typewriters to put together a resume and started sending it out to small newspapers in the Tampa Bay area.

Alcoholic newspaper editors with felony records are not exactly hot commodities — but I had one thing going for me. I could be had cheap. That got me a job with a throwaway weekly in Brooksville — a few pages of local news wrapped around low-cost classified ads and public announcements. I was given an office and a salary that was less than what I had earned as a neophyte reporter. But I had a job.

Waterfront Property

The life of a drinking, low-bottom alcoholic is as predictable as the ticking of a metronome. Promises, hopes, wishes, plans, desires, all built around the simple need not to take a drink, followed by what seems to be the inevitable picking up of the first drink… just one… this time it will be different… I can handle it… followed by the quick skid into what the fellowship describes, rightly, as a "place of loneliness, terror, bewilderment, and despair."

That's why *Groundhog Day* is the perfect movie for an alky. A drunk, a drunk like me, understands that life of constant repetition. "Different day, same shit," is a refrain heard in every bar I've ever been in, and that's a lot of bars. Hell, I lived that life for almost four decades.

I left the Salvation Army determined to build a new life, a life without booze. I got my car and drove to Brooksville where I rented a little trailer on its own plot of land out in the boonies, surrounded by nature. I bought groceries and I went to work.

All was good for about a week. Then one night, as I left the office after working late, I spied the hillbilly beer and wine joint down the street. I could hear the music pouring out of the open front door, hear laughter and conversation. I thought about the drive home to my trailer, thought of sitting there alone, eating some frozen dinner, watching television. I thought of Cathy and Dylan and Eamon. I thought of the nights we were together and at least a little happy. It was as if an invisible hand took me by the shoulder and led me to the bar.

"This time it will be different," I thought. "It will… it really will. I'll just have one beer. Maybe two. Then I'll be fine. I'll feel whole again, connected. Just one beer. Maybe two."

God, that first beer looked beautiful. I held up the glass and looked through the amber liquid at the world. I raised it to my lips and drank deep, so deep that I emptied the glass without taking it down from my lips.

"Give me another beer, bartender!"

I may as well have left town as soon as I drank that first beer, driven to the jail in Dade City, and turned myself in. Once I started drinking, I had no more chance of staying sober and out of lockup than I had of flapping my arms and flying. I got so drunk that night that I couldn't even consider making an attempt to drive home. I let myself back into the office and slept on the floor of the darkroom, waking just before the rest of the staff showed up for work.

For the next six weeks or so, I managed to hold on to the job, while drinking as much as I could and constantly running out of money. I'd go through the desks in the office looking for change. I'd bounce checks anyplace I could find suckers who'd cash them. Finally, after showing up for an interview with the county sheriff so drunk I could hardly walk, I was fired.

I lived on my final paycheck for a few weeks, drinking every day, eating cold canned beans, and watching sitcom reruns on television. The money ran all the way out just about the same time as my car broke down. Desperate, I hitchhiked to Tampa, a bigger city where I figured the panhandling would be easy. I was filthy, unshaven, nauseated. I had scabs all over my arms and legs. My teeth hadn't been brushed in weeks. I had a face that scared small children and wild eyes that unsettled anyone who looked into their madness.

For a time, I lived in a cardboard box under a bridge somewhere in Tampa. I laugh, now, and call that my waterfront property, but there was nothing funny about it. I cadged money wherever I could. I checked every pay phone, hoping to find a few coins in the return slot. I'd sneak into mini-marts to rip off a bottle of cheap wine. I walked miles. Eventually, I came up with a con.

In those days, most bars and restaurants had condom machines in their bathrooms. Working a different neighborhood each day, I'd find a nice place and sidle in. Then I'd start screaming.

"I put three bucks in your rubber machine! Your rubber machine stole my money! Give me my goddam money!"

The flustered manager, confronted by this raging, disgusting idiot almost always handed over a few dollars just to get rid of me.

One morning, I found myself standing in a line outside a rundown building. I stank of urine and wine and the filth I'd been rolling around in. I had no recollection at all of how I came to be in that line or why I was there. I was there, probably, because somebody had told me it was a good place to go. I hoped it was a free kitchen and that I'd get something to eat.

The line shuffled forward.

"Wha… what is this place?" I asked the guy who seemed to be in charge of monitoring the line.

"Are you fuckin' serious?" he answered. "You don't even know where you are?"

I shook my head, hoping it wouldn't fall off my shoulders. I stepped away from the building to get a better look.

"Holy shit!" I said. It was a plasma center — maybe the same one Cathy and I passed that time we took the kids to Busch Gardens — and I was waiting in line for the chance to sell my blood. I remembered what she had said to me: "Keep going and that's where you'll end up."

I gagged and had to lean over and take deep breaths to keep from puking.

"Please," I said, "somebody help me. I need help."

By the end of the day, I was back in the Salvation Army shelter, so weak I couldn't hold a coffee cup, unable to look anyone in the eye. But I was off the street.

I slept in a bed fitted with rubber sheets. I poured sweat as if I'd been running in the sun. I hadn't had anything like a normal shit in weeks, now I had the runs almost ceaselessly. I choked when I tried to eat solid food. One by one, the counselors came in and talked to me. Though they expressed concern, there weren't any hugs and nobody was singing Seals & Crofts. I started shaking and kept shaking for a week, two weeks. Slowly, very slowly, the booze left my system.

"Now what?" I asked the head counselor.

She shook her head sadly. "We've done all we can for you," she said. "We're going to transfer you to the Florida Alcoholism Treatment Center in Avon Park. Maybe they can help."

Her voice made it plain that she didn't think there was much chance of that happening. But the Salvation Army really had done all it could do for me — and more than it had to.

Avon Park was, at the time, considered to have the best alcohol treatment program in the state. But it wasn't all that different from the Salvation Army's. There were groups and classes and lots of singing. "Kumbaya" and "We Shall Overcome" were the songs of choice. And, of course, there were meetings of the fellowship, where we'd sit at the back of the room and listen to the old-timers tell their stories — what life used to be like and what it was like after they got sober. The big difference at Avon Park was that most of the counselors were drunks themselves. Sober drunks, but still drunks.

There was one guy in particular who'd stop by my room after the day's activities were finished to chew the fat. We'd have a smoke as he talked about his days on the street and how he'd created a whole new life for himself when he finally got sober. He hadn't had a drink for almost 20 years.

We really hit it off — and for the first time, I felt like I was talking to somebody who understood what my life was like, what it was like to screw everything up and still want to drink, only to drink, no matter what the cost.

After six weeks at Avon Park, I was sent back to Tampa, to a halfway house where I could live while I found a job and tried to get back on my feet. There were about eight of us in the house, a three-bedroom bungalow not far from the bay, one of the nicest neighborhoods in the city. The house was old but comfortable, with a living room large enough for the in-house program meetings we had several times a week.

After dinner my second or third evening there, I got a phone call. It was the sheriff's lieutenant who'd tipped me off when I was going to be arrested in New Port Richey.

"Listen," he said, "there's a warrant out for your arrest."

"Oh, shit," I said.

"Yeah," he agreed. "Probation violation. We got word from Avon Park that you were in Tampa. I figured I'd let you know."

"What should I do?" I asked.

He didn't answer right away. "I'll tell you the truth," he said. "We're not coming over to a different county to arrest you."

I breathed a bit easier.

"But," he said, "you'll get caught eventually."

He paused. "I think you should turn yourself in. Face the music."

I hung up the phone.

Christ! If I turned myself in, I'd be doing some hard time. Not a couple of months but a year. Maybe more. I needed to think, so I went for a walk along the waterfront. It's a beautiful spot, with large estates on one side of Bayshore Drive and the gentle waters of Tampa Bay on the other.

I kept walking. I left the waterfront and started down a side street. It was dark. The street was empty. Suddenly, ahead, I spotted a red, flashing, neon light shaped like a cocktail glass. On and off. The light seemed to call me. I could imagine the sound of ice cubes dropping into a rocks glass — and I knew what I had to do.

The next day, I got a ride to the sheriff's office in New Port Richey. I turned myself in.

Tight Scrotum

At first, I was held in the county jail, in the same tiny, dirty, overcrowded cell I'd occupied on my first visit. The food still sucked, the coffee was still miserable, the "screws" were surly and nasty as always, but so were the prisoners. It wasn't so bad, though, because I figured this was just a temporary stop on a journey that would end with me in one of the 100 or so prisons and work camps scattered from Pensacola to the Florida Keys. The judge had promised me prison time if I were arrested again, and I didn't see any reason to doubt his word.

As before, I burrowed into this little world knowing the best thing to do was to keep out of sight, mind my own business, stay cool. As an old cock who'd already done some county time, and a felon, I was given grudging respect by the younger guys in the lockup, most of whom were in for short periods on charges like DUI or leaving the scene of an accident.

I took the lower bunk closest to the front of the eight-man cell, where the light and air — such as it was — was a little better. I fashioned a nest for myself, attaching some magazine pictures to the wall with toothpaste (the inmate's Elmer's Glue) and stashing Styrofoam cups and other odds and ends that I thought might be useful. I spent most of my second day grinding an empty soda can on the concrete floor, round and round, till the top was worn off. A string of torn bed sheet tied through little holes poked in the sides of the can gave me a handle so I could hold my "cooker" over a "bomb" — about a quarter of a roll of toilet paper rolled up and set ablaze. Using this apparatus, I could reheat coffee or soup or whatever else I managed to stockpile.

When I sat back in my little space, holding a cup of hot coffee — even the miserable chicory coffee served in the jail — and a smoke, I felt almost human. Not quite, but almost. If I closed my eyes, I could imagine myself somewhere else, anywhere else, until the noise — the noise of steel doors clanging shut, of inmates shouting, howling, weeping, cursing, and praying — intruded to remind me exactly what and where I was.

And that's how I spent the next four months, hidden away in my nest, emerging only for meals.

The day before my hearing, I was given an old suit and a half-decent shirt and told to make myself presentable. The only mirror I had was the flimsy piece of polished aluminum that hung in the cell, no more reflective than a tin can. As a consequence, I had no idea how I looked when I was taken from the jail to the court for sentencing. I knew my teeth were bad. I knew I was skinny, that I'd lost weight on the crappy jailhouse diet. I knew I was unkempt. Another inmate had cut my hair with a pair of dull scissors provided by a jailer and I'd shaved in cold water with no shave cream. But I was shocked when I was allowed to use the bathroom at the courthouse and saw myself in a real mirror.

My skin was gray, my eyes dull and staring. I had dark circles under my eyes and sunken cheeks. I grinned a kind of skull's head grin and saw yellow teeth and receding gums. It wasn't just the time in jail, it was the drinking, the months of living on the street, the lack of food, the cheap, sweet wine.

"Oh, Christ, what have I done to myself? Sweet Jesus Fuck!"

I remembered walking into a low-life bar years ago, grabbing a seat on a stool and catching sight of myself in the back-bar mirror.

"Who the hell is that ugly bastard?" I wondered.

With a shock, I realized I was looking at myself. I looked away, looked instead at the shot of tequila I'd ordered. I tossed it off and signaled for another. Then another. After three or four hookers of tequila, I raised my head and looked again in the mirror. God, I was handsome! Broad-shouldered. Ready for action. A regular rock star. Bring on the women! I winked at my image and ordered another drink.

But in the courthouse bathroom, there was no tequila.

The sentencing itself was short and sweet.

"Mr. Doherty," said the judge — that same judge! — "you do realize that you face a maximum of 50 years in prison."

In the time I'd spent as a reporter, sitting in the press row about a dozen feet behind where I now stood, I'd noticed that whenever a man stood before a judge about to drop the hammer of justice, he invariably clenched his hands behind his back, tightening his grip at the moment of sentencing until his fingers turned white. It made no difference the crime — it could be murder or a misdemeanor. It made no difference the criminal — he could be a cringing coward arrested for trying to pick up some undercover cop or a truly badass member of a motorcycle gang. I was no exception. When the judge looked over the top of his glasses at me and said that I faced 50 years, I felt my scrotum tighten and my cock shrink as if I'd stepped into a freezing pond. My hands clenched behind my back and I'm sure my fingers turned white.

"Fifty years," I thought. "Holy shit. I guess that's right. Two felonies per check. Ten felonies all told. Five years for each one. That's 50 years."

I prayed to God the only way I knew how: "Hey, man, cut me a break."

But He didn't.

"Mr. Doherty," the judge intoned. "This saddens me. I've known you as a journalist welcome in my court. I've known you socially. I've given you every opportunity to salvage your life. Now it's come to this. Reluctantly, I sentence you to five years on each count."

I held my breath.

"Five years on each count," he repeated, "with each sentence to run concurrent."

I let my breath out as the bailiff moved to stand beside me.

I was told I'd be bused to the Lake Butler Correctional Institution in the morning, the maximum security "welcoming" facility where I'd be held until it was determined where I'd be permanently placed. I had to, as they say, pack my shit.

"You can make a call, if you want," one of the guards said, with more sensitivity than I had a right to expect. I nodded and a pay phone was wheeled in.

I made the call collect. My father answered the phone. When the operator told him who was calling, there was a moment of silence before he agreed to accept the charges. I don't remember exactly what I said, but I know I told him that I'd been sentenced and was going to state prison. I told him I'd write. I don't remember the exact words he used, but he told me that he and my mother were changing their wills so my sons would get anything that was left when they died, not me. I almost laughed. "Who gives a shit," I thought. "I'm going to prison."

"Can I talk to Mom?" I asked.

I imagined my old man sitting at the big, round table in the family room of the house he and my mother had built after they retired. I imagined his face closed tight as a fist, his ice-blue eyes unblinking. God, he could be a hard man, hard as flint. I imagined him holding the phone in my mother's direction. There was a long pause. It was so long I thought we'd been disconnected.

Finally, my father said, "Your mother won't talk to you. She said to tell you that if you were on fire she wouldn't piss on you to put it out."

SOBERING UP
(SORT OF)
IN MAXIMUM
SECURITY

One Day at a Time

On the bus ride to Lake Butler, I asked an old con for some advice. I asked if he thought I'd be sent to Raiford, the worst of the state prisons and, in fact, one of the worst prisons in the country.

"Nah," he told me. "Your crime isn't serious enough to get you sent to the Rock."

"Do I have to worry about... about... you know?"

He knew what I meant. He grinned.

"I don't figure," he said. "You're too old and ugly for that."

"Listen," he said, "everything depends on how you carry yourself. Don't take any shit from anybody, right from day one. Don't borrow anything. Don't lend anything. Don't talk to the screws unless you have to or everybody will think you're a rat. Have one good friend who'll take your back, and you take his. And remember, if you carry yourself like a bitch, somebody'll turn you into a bitch. Walk like a man."

My first day at the Lake Butler prison, after the long bus ride, after the welcoming speech from Cellblock Slim, standing naked in the freezing north wind along with the other guys from the bus, I didn't feel like a man. I felt like a little kid. I felt like crying.

Eventually we were led into a building where we were relieved of all our personal possessions except for wallets, smokes, and whatever money we had over 20 dollars. We were handed a pair of gray fatigues, white boxer shorts and a T-shirt, white socks, and a jacket.

After slipping into our new clothes, we were led into a huge room filled with wooden benches. A long counter ran across the front of the room. One side wall was solid windows overlooking the prison yard, where I could see hundreds of prisoners walking slowly in circles. The other side wall was comprised of a line of small cells fitted with floor-to-ceiling roller bars.

I watched as two guards carrying automatic rifles at the ready walked a shackled prisoner across the front of the room to the cells, swung the door to one of them open, and pushed the man in. I remembered what Slim had said: "Inside this place, there is another place that is twice as bad." I wondered what the guy had done to be put in jail inside a prison.

From there, we were led to a cellblock set aside to temporarily house us. It was a square building with three tiers of cells facing a floor-to-ceiling open area, sort of like an atrium. A railed walkway ran along the front of each tier of cells, paced by a guard swinging a club. We were taken up to the top tier and assigned one-man cells.

"Move in," the guard said. "Stand clear."

I walked into my cell, a tiny space about five feet wide and eight feet long, with a toilet at one end. "Close!" I heard the guard shout Instantly, the barred doors on all the cells on the tier rumbled shut.

"Here we go," I thought.

For the next three days, we were held in the cellblock, taken out every day and herded into a reception area where we were given physical exams, psychological tests, poked, prodded, questioned, insulted, and finally given prison numbers, fully initiating us into the brotherhood of the convict.

We were told not to forget our number, never to forget it. This number, we were told, took the place of our name. When we heard it called out, we were to immediately respond. It was to be included as an integral part of our name and address in any correspondence sent to us or by us.

I swore that I would, indeed, never forget my prison number. And for years, I did remember it. Now I find that I've forgotten it. I think that's a good thing. But I haven't forgotten that when my father wrote me letters while I was in prison — one a month, like clockwork — he did not write "Dear Kieran" or "Dear Son." He wrote "Dear... " whatever my prison number was.

I was transferred from that cellblock to one of a series of large open-bay cellblocks that faced the prison yard like school dormitories around a quad. Each of those cellblocks housed about 140 men in two sleeping areas, complete with bunk beds and metal lockers. An inmate's bunk and locker was his "house" — a little corner of the world he could consider his own space, a space that was, of course, anything but private.

A central guard station sat between the two sleeping areas, along with a small day room with a television set and a large latrine fitted with toilets, urinals, sinks, and showers. The guard station was a glass and steel enclosure that allowed the guards — male and female — to observe all the action in the sleeping areas, day room, and even the latrine.

The day began with a body count. We sat on our bunks as the guards walked by, physically counting every one of us. That was followed by the morning meal, usually eggs, grits, toast, coffee, and milk. Each inmate was issued a plastic cup to use during his time behind bars. Most of us ran our belt through our cup handle to make sure we didn't lose our treasure. Like all our meals, breakfast was eaten off a metal tray with a spoon, there were no knives or forks.

After breakfast, we went on to the open yard. There were no seats, none at all, only closely trimmed grassy areas surrounded by sidewalks that seemed to lead nowhere. We were expected to keep moving, not to stop anywhere for any length of time, and to make sure we did not step on the grass.

Hour after hour, I walked, my hands in my pockets, looking down at the ground. If I'd stop and lean against a wall, just for a moment, some brown-uniformed guard would holler to keep moving... keep moving. When I stopped, I couldn't help but look at the gun towers that stood watch over the yard, tall as corn silos, each one with a mirrored glass and a raised platform where a machine-gun toting guard surveyed the inmates below.

The meaningless routine of walking and walking was broken by the noon meal, sandwiches, and Kool-Aid that, it was rumored, was pissed in by some pissed off con in the kitchen. After the noon meal, we were shunted into our cellblocks to once again sit on our bunks for a body count. When that was done, it was back to the yard and the walking. If you had an appointment with a doctor or counselor or chaplain, a loudspeaker squawked your prison number and name, usually three times, no more. If you missed your appointment, too bad. There was no real urgency. You weren't going anywhere.

The only entertainment in the yard was watching the flocks of seagulls that flew in every morning to attack the garbage behind the mess hall, then ceaselessly circle the yard — little, feathered, black-and-white, beaked inmates, cawing as they searched for scraps, cigarette butts, who knows what. In the evening, as the sun lowered in the west, the flock would rise, thousands of birds moving as one, to head again toward where? The gulf? The ocean? Some nearby lake? Nobody knew.

Before dinner, there was another body count, followed by a meal of liver or mullet or stew made of some unidentifiable ingredients, along with the omnipresent grits and beans. Then we were marched, as a group, back to our cellblock. The next two hours or so were spent writing letters or just sitting around waiting for the time to pass.

For two months, I lived from day to day, waiting to find out where they would end up placing me. Finally, I was called into the office of one of the prison's counselors. He told me that because I was nonviolent and because I could type — a valuable commodity in a system largely run on inmate labor — I could choose to go to pretty much any prison in the state.

"You can get close to your home, if you want," he, said. "You can go to a road camp or a minimum security prison. It's up to you."

I had no idea what to say. He spoke as if he were truly interested in me and my future. I guessed he'd gone to college to get a degree to help people, unlike most of the screws who were recruited from the huge body of rednecks in rural Florida. I also figured he'd only been at the prison a short while, not long enough to lose his idealistic dream of doing some good.

"What do you think?" I asked.

He nodded.

"I think you should stay here," he said. "It's a quiet place. It's maximum security, but the inmates who are permanent here aren't looking to make reps."

In other words, while I'd still be under armed guard, there was an upside. The prison population that basically ran the institution was comprised of men who weren't likely to be violent. That was worth a lot.

I took his advice.

"Permanent Party" Inmate

I became a "permanent party" inmate at Lake Butler and was given a job as a clerk in a warehouse where all the food and other supplies for the prison were delivered by outside contractors. I was issued a white uniform to differentiate me from the gray-clad temporary inmates. I was assigned a "house" in the permanent inmate cellblock, a large building with two open-bay dormitories, a day room, classrooms, a small library, a hobby shop, and, of course, a central guard station.

My life quickly settled into a routine. Count in the morning, followed by breakfast. Then free time for about an hour. After that, I'd join a crew of about a half-dozen men who walked from the cellblock to a gatehouse where two guards kept watch. We were searched for contraband, sometimes just a simple pat down but often a drop-trousers strip-search. Once we were cleared through the gate, we gathered on the street outside the prison. A guard met us and marched us about a half-block to the warehouse. As we walked along what was basically a rural, dirt road, the men in the gun towers watched us, their weapons ready to fire. I often wondered how hard they prayed for one of us to break from the pack and run.

I was required to work in the warehouse for about three hours in the morning and three in the afternoon. My job was to take care of the accounts for a civilian who was in charge of supplying cigarettes, candy, and other sundries to all the canteens in the prison system. From the first day, the civilian, I'll call him Mr. W., and I hit it off.

"How long do you think it will take you to get the books in order and keep them in order?" he asked after I'd been working in his office for about a week. "Honestly."

The accounts, which had been kept for years by inmates who didn't much give a shit, really were a mess. Even so, I figured getting them straightened out would not be a full-time job.

"Honestly?" I asked.

He nodded.

"I could get them squared away in less than six months," I said.

He nodded.

"Halfa day each day should give me plenty of time," I added.

Mr. W. knew from my records that I'd been a journalist and he knew I could type. He was smart enough to figure that I would like time to do some work for myself. He also knew better than I how the prison operated.

"You work a half-day for me and give me honest work," he said, "and you can use the typewriter and other supplies and work the other half-day for yourself.

I knew what a break I was getting. Not just because I worked inside, in an office, with a civilian, but also because I had been handed a way to make money. And everybody in the joint needed some way to make money, to take part in the prison's thriving underground economy.

I quickly went into business typing legal documents for my fellow inmates — requests for new hearings, divorce papers, and petitions — at the going rate of a dollar a page. I also wrote term papers for inmates who were taking courses at the in-prison junior college. And I made a deal with the operator of the prison canteen. Every day, I'd place an order for candy, cookies, and sodas that he would bring to me in the block after the canteen closed at 7:00 p.m. Then I'd open my "store," selling items for a dime more than their canteen price. In a good evening, I'd clear five bucks.

Other inmates had their own things going. Those who worked full-time as cooks earned money — usually a dollar a day from each customer — smuggling hot sandwiches to inmates with cash who didn't want to eat the muck served to the other convicts. One inmate in my cellblock, an old black man, flitted around at night dressed in women's underwear, including a bra stuffed with rolled up socks, and a pair of pumps. For a quarter a day, he made my bed and swept around my area.

The guards were aware of what was going on, but they turned a blind eye to just about any activity — including the sexual ones — provided the inmates didn't get too rowdy. After all, they had nothing to worry about. They could always bust anyone who became a troublemaker.

So the days passed, one after another, astonishing in their sameness. I'd wake at 6:00 a.m. to the sound of a guard walking along the rows of bunks and slamming the end of each one with a nightstick. I'd make a cup of instant coffee. After count, I'd go outside and sit where I could look through the fence at a wooded area filled with pines and old, moss-hung oaks. I'd eat my breakfast sandwich there, then get ready for work.

At midday, after working on Mr. W.'s books, I'd come back to the prison and check for mail at the special "legal mail" mail room. I never got any legal mail, never expected any, but it passed the time. Then I'd go to the cellblock for count and wait for my lunch sandwich to be delivered. In the afternoon, I worked for myself or, if I didn't have any work to do, read one of the books that Mr. W. brought me from time to time. At the end of the day, it was back inside for yet another count and another delivered sandwich.

After the evening meal, we were on our own. Some inmates went to the college classes that were offered. Some went to a hobby area where they could make wallets, belts, some wooden items, or just sniff glue to get high. Others went to the small library of ancient books housed inside the block. Most, and I was one, simply hung out, smoking, drinking coffee, writing letters, or simply lying about their criminal or sexual exploits. At 9:00 p.m., there was another count and then, soon after that, lights out, except for the constant glow from the guard station and the reflection of sweeping searchlights inching their way across the walls and ceiling.

Weekends were much the same, only without work. I found that I could sleep all day Saturday and Sunday, waking only for counts and meals and to run my shop. I think the reason I was able to do it was because my body and mind cried out for the escape. And so I slept.

There were, of course, a lot of rules that had to be followed. I had to shave every day. Turn in my sheets once weekly and uniforms no more than three times a week. Shirts had to be tucked in at all times. No facial hair. No phone calls, none at all other than legal calls. All letters — incoming and outgoing — were censored. No dirty books or pictures. No inmate could have more than 20 dollars in cash at any time. And so on.

Most of these rules were observed just because it was easier to toe the line than to hassle with the guards. The cash limit rule caused me some problems until I found a couple of guys who would hold money for me for a fee, usually a dollar week. One of them usually managed to slip my money to his wife, who then deposited it in a bank for me.

There were also rules that went beyond the rules put in place by the prison. Don't act friendly to a guard, no matter what. If one tries to engage you in conversation, don't talk unless there's a witness. Don't look in another man's eyes unless you're ready to challenge him or be challenged. And whatever you do, don't ever, ever show weakness. Protect your own property. Keep your hands to yourself. Don't ask personal questions. Never ask another man what his crime is. Carry yourself like a man. If you look afraid, you're dead meat.

Trust was a big part of life inside the joint. And the convicts I knew were among some of the most trustworthy men I ever met. If I gave my buddy 50 dollars to slip to his wife, that's what he did. If I gave a man a dollar to hold 20 dollars for me, he would no more think of stealing it than he would think of attacking a guard. And it wasn't just a matter of "honor among thieves." As every inmate knew, being labeled a thief or a rat could have nasty — even deadly — consequences.

One of the men whose bunk was close to mine was a murderer close to release after spending more than two decades in lockup. He wasn't real friendly, but he did nod in my direction each time we passed. I watched him. He was mostly silent, but made it plain that he would take no crap from anybody. When he did speak, he spoke softly. Other inmates treated him with deference. He minded his own business. He became my role model.

I fully expected to spend no more than a year in prison. After all, my crime was nonviolent, almost laughable. Sure, I'd forged five checks — but, really, my take was only 38 dollars. Chump change. So from day one, I started keeping track of the days, marking them in pencil on the side of my locker. One day, my role model asked me what I was doing. I told him.

"That'll make you crazy as shit," he said. "Don't even think about it. Just do your time one day at a time."

It took some practice, but I got good at doing just what he said. I'd break my day down into manageable pieces with a reward for each piece completed. Wake up. Make it through morning count and then have a cup of coffee outside, looking at the trees. Work, then take a little walk to the legal mail room. Lie down until count. Work, with a break for one of the snacks that Mr. W. provided. Back to the cellblock for a nap until count. Wake for dinner. Read until count. (I got good at masturbating quietly, too.)

And so the days passed.

It was almost a year before I got to see the parole board. All that time, I was expecting to be released at any moment. But when I finally met the board, they slapped me with the news that each of my five counts of forgery was being considered as a completely separate crime. That meant that while I could expect to do about one year for the first count, each successive count added time to my sentence. I was told, in effect, that I'd be doing as much time as some bank robbers, just a bit less than some murderers.

Luckily, I was given credit for all my county jail time and had been earning "gained time" by staying out of trouble in the prison. Still, I ended up doing nearly three years for 38 dollars — making the drinks I bought with that money expensive beyond belief.

Then, early one morning, I was awakened by a guard hitting the bars of my cell with a nightstick.

"Wake up, inmate. You're for work release in Miami."

Click-Click

For the next seven months, I served my time in a work release center in Miami. At first, I found a job with a sportswear manufacturing company, in an office, entering orders into a computer. I was half convict, half free man, working in the world each day, taking buses, eating in fast-food joints, flirting inexpertly with co-workers, then returning to the prison — a motel-like collection of buildings not far from the Miami Airport — at night.

I had plenty of opportunities to drink. There was always liquor in the work release center, carried in by men like me who spent all day working outside. My roommate, a big hillbilly who worked in a restaurant, stayed drunk most of the time. He'd lie in his bed, cradling a bottle of Black Jack. He'd offer me a hit and then laugh when I said no.

"You'll be drunk as soon as you get out," he said. "I know your type."

There were times when I salivated like a hungry dog over a T-bone at the thought-memory of booze sliding down my gullet and hitting the switch in my head that made me feel that everything was okay — "click-click." But I didn't take the bait.

I'd been sober for three years, and I felt physically better than I had in years. I'd gained back some of the weight lost when I was in the county jail and I was even saving money. I'd saved an incredible $2,000 while I was locked up, the first time I'd ever saved a dime. In work release, after paying the state for my upkeep, I had a couple of hundred dollars a week left and I put that in the bank too. It added up to almost $8,000. Hell, if my sentence had been long enough, I would have had enough to retire.

Still, there was no real commitment to sobriety on my part, no real willingness to face what being sober meant in terms of facing demons and making changes. I'd stay sober as long as I really wanted to, then we'd see what happened. That was my unspoken promise to myself. In the meantime, though I couldn't admit it to myself, fear is what kept me from drinking. I was terrified that if I drank, I'd get caught and be shipped back to prison, real prison.

A couple of months before my full release, when I'd grown tired of the repetitive and mostly mindless work at a computer, I started looking for a writing job. With the good fortune I didn't usually experience, I heard of an opening at International Voyager Publishing, one of the nation's most successful travel publishing companies. I applied for the job, passed a simple writing test, and was scheduled to be interviewed by the company's owner, a young Englishman named Peter Saville.

Peter was one of the brightest men I'd ever met. He'd taken a one-magazine company and built it into an operation that provided in-cabin magazines to almost every cruise ship sailing from the port of Miami. He produced travel films for cruise lines and hotels and provided hardbound guidebooks to every major hotel in the Caribbean. He was also easygoing about everything but making money.

I knew I'd have to tell Peter the truth, that I was a convict in work release, because he had to understand that, for the time being, there was no way I could work late or weekends. When he gestured for me to take a seat in his office, I sat and immediately started talking.

"I'm in prison," I said, running my words together.

He nodded.

"Work release," I said. "I'd like to explain."

"I only have one question," he said.

"What's that?"

"Did you kill your mother or father?"

"No."

"Well, you can write," he said. "And that's all I care about."

I was hired, making more money than I'd ever earned before as a journalist. I was put in charge of a project to produce a hardbound travel book for the hotels in St. Thomas. My job was to do research in Miami, come up with an outline, then, after my full release, go to the island for a month or six weeks to pull together the rest of what I'd need to write the book. While there, I'd be given a complimentary room at Bluebeard's Castle, one of the island's resort hotels, free food, an expense account, and a rented car. It sounded great!

As the time neared for my release, I wrote an article that was published in the Sunday magazine section of the *Miami Herald* — and made the mistake of ridiculing some of the guards at the work release center. As a result, my remaining time there was made more difficult. I was subjected to sudden drug tests, searched more diligently, questioned more closely about the money I earned. Still, the days passed.

A few days before I would be moving back into the free world, I rented a bungalow in Miami, a nice place with wooden floors and a fireplace. Meanwhile, International Voyager Publishing made arrangements for me to fly from Miami to Charlotte Amalie, and I packed my bags. I was released at 9:00 a.m., walked out the door to a waiting cab, and, by 10:00 a.m., was on a jet bound for the Caribbean.

I had never in my life seen a place as beautiful as St. Thomas looked from the air. The island's verdant mountains stretched above a sea every bit as turquoise blue as the travel brochures promised. I could hardly believe that just a few hours earlier I'd been a prison inmate, stuck in a work release center not far from the slums of Miami. If I'd had any sense, I'd have counted my blessings. How many convicts leave the joint and fly to one of the most famous resorts in the world?

My sense of wonder continued. I checked into the hotel and found myself in a room facing Charlotte Amalie harbor, looking down on the old city and the red-brick hulk of Fort Christian, built in 1666 to guard the waterfront. Cruise ships lined up along the harbor's main pier, disgorging tourists who ran from shop to shop, from one sightseeing stop to another, sweatily enjoying themselves. Sailboats swung at anchor. Traffic moved noisily along the main harbor road.

Free at last! Thank God Almighty!

I unpacked and headed to the hotel's main dining room to eat my first free-world meal in almost five years, a meal I'd eat with an honest-to-God knife and fork! A waitress was going to give me coffee and ask if wanted a refill. I could go to the bathroom and close the door before I took a crap!

All was well until I walked through the restaurant's front door and found myself in a cocktail lounge — a lounge I'd have to pass through to get a meal. And I heard a man sitting at the bar order a drink.

"Let me have a rum and pineapple, please," he said.

I never drank rum. I hated the taste of pineapple juice. But those words — rum and pineapple — stopped me in my tracks.

"Rum and pineapple," I thought. "I bet I could have one of those, maybe two."

I pictured a tall glass filled with ice cubes that tinkled musically and the heavenly sunshine gold color of pineapple juice with, of course, a touch of rum.

"Hell," I said to myself, "I can have just one. It's been three years. Don't I de-serve a reward for that?"

I sat at the bar.

"Let me have a rum and pineapple, please," I said. "I have time for just one, maybe two before dinner."

I looked at the glass the barman set in front of me. God, it was beautiful. My hand shook a bit as I raised it to my lips.

Son-of-a-bitch that felt good!

Click-click! The switch was hit.

I never did make it into the restaurant. At midnight, I stumbled back to my room. The barman had refused to serve me any more liquor. I hadn't gotten into a fight. I hadn't been loud or abusive. I was simply too drunk.

No fool, I called the concierge from my room and asked if I could get some booze delivered to my room. With his help, I hired a cab to drive to the 24-hour duty-free liquor store at the airport and pick up five fifths of rum.

BACK TO THE BOTTOM

What Can I Say?

You know what happened next.

I began drinking every day, as much as I could and still manage to do something loosely resembling work. The bars in the hotel were open almost around the clock, so I'd start my morning by swilling beer or Bloody Marys by the pool, enough to handle the shakes. Then I'd drive to town, half-drunk already, to do research for the book, scribbling incomprehensible notes about the island's shops and restaurants and history. Late afternoon, I'd end up in a bar at the foot of the mountain road leading to the hotel, drinking rum and ogling the tourist girls in their bathing suits. Then I'd make my way back to my room to pass out, waking in time to force myself to eat something before heading to one of the hotel bars.

I swilled booze and beer in one of the most beautiful spots on earth, paying no attention to anything but my drinking even as my life continued its inexorable decline. Suffering from what I call Rummy's Paranoia, I thought Sydney Greenstreet was following me from bar to bar, spying, reporting to my boss back in Miami. I drove my rented car, too drunk to walk, squinting, closing one eye to make the three roads I saw merge into one.

Once, passed out in my room, I pissed in my bed. Jolted awake by the maid's loud knock on my door, I panicked.

"Just a minute!" I yelled.

I jumped into the shower, fully clothed. Dripping, I tore the sheets off the bed, flipped the mattress, and opened the door. I tipped the maid outrageously to hold her tongue.

During my time in St. Thomas, I signed for thousands of dollars on my room's account — until the hotel manager cut me off, saying I had overspent the amount they'd agreed to trade for a free write-up in the guidebook. Then I started spending the money I'd saved and blew through almost the entire $8,000. But, God, I was king of the hill, living the high life, buying drinks for the house, throwing tips to anybody who looked my way, invincible until my blood alcohol dropped to 0.9 or less and then I started crying, shaking uncontrollably, terrified of life, of the future, of myself.

Out of money, I had no choice but to go back to Miami and get the book done in the office.

In the States, I fell into a routine much like the one I'd had when I was a newspaperman. I'd drink in the morning before work, slip out and have a few drinks at lunch, hang on until the end of the day, then stop in a neighborhood dive, get half shitfaced, and go home to finish the job.

The writing wasn't very challenging, so I didn't have to be completely sober to do it. Mostly, I relied heavily on my ability to quickly "rewrite" — i.e., steal — the work of other writers. Once a month I had to be sober enough to meet with my parole officer, but other than that I could pretty much do as I wished. I had no car, so I couldn't drive drunk. I had no woman in my life. No friends. Not even a pet. Once again, my life was all about the booze.

During the next six months or so, I did two more guidebooks for the company — one for Grand Cayman and one for St. Martin — somehow managing to shake my way through the writing. My trips to both islands passed in a foggy blur. I tried to pick up women and couldn't, was too drunk to masturbate. When I walked, I thought the sidewalk was sloping downward in front of me, forcing me to step gingerly, carefully, as if I were about to fall. I tripped over curbs and walked into trees. I went to a doctor in St. Martin, convinced I had Dengue Fever. He gave me sugar pills.

No matter where I was, my loneliness, my separateness from other people, seemed palpable. Who wants to talk to desperation? I felt transparent, that other people could see me for exactly what I was — a fraud, a liar, a loser, a drunken bum. And yet, I had to maintain this pose, this damned tight-assed pose, as if everything in my life were fine, as if I felt the way everybody else looked.

My guts burned, I hadn't taken anything like a normal crap in months, I went days without eating solid food then wolfed down pickled eggs and hot dogs and sausages and pickled pigs' feet in a bar. My head ached constantly. If I went more than a couple of hours without a drink, my hands shook so badly I couldn't hold a pen. I couldn't remember where I'd been or to whom I'd spoken from one day to the next.

If you think the life of a drinking alky is a life with no responsibility, think again. It's hard work trying to convince the world that you're alive when inside you're all dust and broken bones and congealed blood.

A Loony Surrounded by Loonies

Finally, it came to a head.

I stopped going to work. Alone in my little cottage in Miami, my paranoia grew and grew. I was terrified of sounds, imagined black men crawling across my lawn to break through my door and slit my throat. When the phone rang, I jumped and didn't answer it. Twice, three times an hour, I crabbed my way to my front windows with a butcher knife between my teeth, a fugitive on the lookout for his enemies.

I tried to kill myself. I put my head in the small oven in my kitchen, forgetting that I'd neglected to pay the gas bill. I passed out there, then awoke with lines on my right cheek from the oven rack and a crick in my neck. I wept because I was still alive. I left the cottage to buy a case of booze. But the minute I got home, I nailed the doors shut and crawled under the bed with a bottle, terrified.

A day or a week later, I'm not sure, two people from the office came by and forced the front door open.

"Kieran," one of them hollered, nervously. "We're friends. Don't be frightened!"

They found me cowering under the bed, unshaven, dirty, wearing shitty underwear and a vomit-stained T-shirt, babbling to myself. The next thing I knew, I was in the psychiatric ward at Jackson Hospital.

I was a patient at Jackson, surrounded by loonies, for about two weeks. For most of the first week, I lay in bed and shook. Slowly, helped by frequent doses of a tranquilizer, I came out of it. Though it takes only about 72 hours to rid the body of alcohol, I'd done so much damage to myself that it would be a while before I was completely free of tremors. For months, I itched as if tiny bugs were crawling over my skin. And it was almost a year before I could keep myself from weeping at the sight of a little boy who reminded me of Dylan or a couple, a man and woman, holding hands and happy.

As soon as I was considered to be detoxed, I was seen by a psychiatrist. And I knew that they wouldn't let me out of the loony bin until I convinced him that I wasn't a threat to myself.

We talked as I sat on my bed with my hands clenched together between my knees, trying to hide the shaking. He explained that my hospitalization had been arranged by Peter, my boss, who was, as it turned out, a friend of the head of neuropsychiatry at the hospital. I was on the psych ward for a rest, the doctor said. Just for a rest. Happy to look down on the other patients on the ward, typical grandiosity for an alky, I was relieved when I learned I didn't have to take part in group sessions or weave any baskets or take part in scream therapy.

I wasn't really crazy, the doctor said — maybe a little crazy, but my main problem was that I was an alcoholic.

"When you leave here," he said, "I strongly suggest that you go to Alcoholics Anonymous."

I was feeling pretty good, having been told by an expert that I wasn't really crazy. Then the next day, as I was walking down the corridor, an unshaven brute of a man, clad in a hospital gown, came toward me, smoking six cigarettes at once, three held in each hand. He hissed at me like a snake.

"You!" he said. "I want to talk to you! I can tell we're a lot alike. Yeah, we're a lot alike. We should be friends."

I almost ran back to my room.

Drowning in Rocky Mountain Spring Water

I'd like to say that I was able to stay sober from that day on, but I can't. When I got out of the hospital, I told myself that I had to make a real effort this time, but I honestly didn't know how in hell I was supposed to survive without booze. How could I watch a football game on television without a beer? How could I possibly date or get laid without booze? How could I fill my hours? How could I be charming, talkative, creative? How could I write the great novel I had inside me? Never mind that I was never charming, talkative, or particularly creative. Never mind that I'd never seriously started any novel, let alone a great one.

I forced myself to go to AA meetings, but it took years for me to find a way to make the fellowship's 12 Steps and Traditions work for me. At first, I didn't see how they would help me stay sober. What really turned me off, though, was all the God talk. Some members talked about a "higher power," but I knew they were really talking about God, a God I couldn't or wouldn't believe in.

I'd stand up at the end of a meeting and say the formulaic words: "I'm Kieran, and I'm an alcoholic." People applauded, but I still felt like an outsider. I didn't understand the lingo. There were signs and posters all over the place. "One Day at a Time." "Keep It Simple." "HALT." During a break, I asked the guy next to me what HALT meant. He told me it meant I shouldn't let myself get too hungry, angry, lonely, or tired. I could have sworn he said I shouldn't let myself get too "horny," angry, lonely, or tired, so I grinned like an idiot. Then I wondered why he looked at me like I'd crawled out from under a rock.

I had to admit, though, it felt pretty good being in that room, in a place where it seemed people understood me even if I didn't understand them.

For the next 10 years — for the first time in my adult life — I managed to function almost like a normal human being. I was working for myself, freelancing, and I was making pretty good money.

I was sober much of the time, but slipped back into drinking after staying away from booze for one year or two or maybe three. Usually, there was no "reason" I could think of to justify my picking up a drink and getting drunk. I just did it. Once, I was enticed by an ad campaign announcing that Coors Beer — brewed with "pure Rocky Mountain spring water" — was now available in Florida. That was a big deal. For years, many years, Coors was sold only west of the Mississippi.

Jesus. I would see one of those ads on TV and close my eyes, wondering, just wondering, what Coors beer tasted like. I'd open my eyes and in a few minutes or an hour I'd see another Coors ad. And I'd think, "I've gotten drunk on beer. Hell, I've gotten drunk on Bud and Schlitz and Meister Brau and Kirin in Japan and Carta Blanca in Mexico. But I've never gotten drunk on Coors. I bet," I'd think, "that Coors is different. I bet that Rocky Mountain spring water makes Coors different. I bet I can drink some Coors and be okay. Drink some Coors and not get drunk thanks to the Rocky Mountain spring water."

I'd gotten into the habit of taking a morning walk to a little magazine store where I'd buy *The New York Times* and a pack or two of Camel smokes. Along the way, I passed the only tavern in the neighborhood, a tavern that opened its doors at about 8:00 a.m., a tavern where the smell of beer and booze washed through the opened doors and swept over me as I walked past. With Coors constantly on my mind, I couldn't help but think of going in and ordering one. Just one. To see what it tasted like. To see if it really was different.

Then one morning, as I approached the bar with *The New York Times* under my arm and a fresh pack of Camels in my pocket, I stopped. I took a deep breath, walked through the open doors, sat down on one of the empty stools, and ordered a Coors.

"I'll bet I don't get drunk," I thought as the bartender put the glass in front of me.

I drank and the worst thing possible happened. I loved the taste. And when the glass was empty, I put it down, stood up, and walked home.

"Shit," I thought, "I'm not an alky. I just had one beer and stopped."

The next day, I went into the bar and had one beer and went home. On the third day, I went in and had two, but I was still okay. I didn't get drunk. The fourth day was the one. On the fourth day, I went into the bar, ordered a Coors, and, as I drank it, spied a half-full bottle of Jose Cuervo at the back bar. I pulled five 20-dollar bills out of my wallet and put them down in front of me.

"Bring me that bottle of Jose Cuervo," I said. "Just leave it here and keep the hundred."

I sat there for about four hours, drinking that tequila with beer back-ups, growing drunker and drunker, and, by God, loving it.

It ended with me in a treatment center — and no idea how I'd gotten there.

Then I met — actually, re-met — Lynne.

REWRITING
THE END

Lynne

Like I said, I was freelancing, writing business articles and producing a weekly stock index for Florida newspapers. (It was not unlike the Dow Jones Industrial Average but was based on trading activity in 30 Florida companies.) I had more work than I could comfortably handle by myself — and I remembered a young woman, Lynne Furet, I'd known as a newspaper writer, not extensively published but with enough experience to help me out. I found her number, called, and asked if she was interested in doing a couple of articles for me. She said yes, and we set a time to meet at a Burger King not far from her house.

I don't remember anything about the articles I wanted her to do. What I do remember is how wonderful she looked as she walked into the restaurant and over to the table where I was sitting. She was — is — one of the most beautiful women I've ever seen, not unlike Princess Diana only with a more engaging smile. She's older now, of course — almost 20 years older — but I still regard her the same way.

That meeting was October 15, 1990. We started dating soon afterward, got engaged on Christmas Day, and married on April 12,1991.

By the time we married, I was approaching two years of sobriety. Lynne knew I was a sober drunk. She'd gone to fellowship meetings with me, had listened to me talk about my past as an invited speaker at meetings in Miami.

When we got married, I figured I'd never drink again. She hoped I wouldn't. We both very much wanted to believe in "happily ever after." Neither one of us expected this story to end the way it now appears it will.

When I started this memoir about two years ago, I had just been diagnosed with terminal lung cancer.

Lynne and I had been married for 16 years and I had been sober for 14 — some of them pretty rough. But we'd made it through. Now, I believed I could forecast the end of my days. I saw myself growing weaker and thinner, sinking into some kind of hospice care and then dying, drugged to my gills and out of consciousness and pain. Lynne, my darling wife, would be at my side during all those days, kneeling by my bed as I drew my last breath.

I was so sure that's the way my life would end that I even wrote it up as the final chapter of this book. But I've had to keep rewriting that chapter because so much has been changing from day to day. The biggest challenge Lynne and I have had to deal with: a flare-up of her mental illness… almost certainly caused by having to face the ugly reality that I'm dying.

Just as Lynne was aware of my alcoholism and accepted the risks when we got married, I knew she was sick and accepted those risks — but I had no idea she could suffer as terribly as she has in the last two years. Some doctors say she has bipolarism, periods of horrible, depressive fear followed by periods of unbelievable, manic happiness. Other doctors have given her the more serious diagnosis of "schizo-affective disorder." In the past two years, Lynne has been hospitalized five times, for a total of 10 weeks. There was improvement after each hospitalization, but only for a time.

Having to go through treatment for a lethal illness as I attempt to help my wife is brutal. Following chemo, I am often so weak and nauseated that I am virtually useless around the house and around Lynne. Time that I need to rest and recover, I have been forced to spend trying to keep our lives somehow concrete when everything seems to be crashing into pieces.

A few weeks ago, driving to visit my wife in the mental hospital, I realized I would have to reschedule my chemotherapy for the following week so I could sit in on the next hearing to determine if she should be released.

"Shit," I thought.

That's right. I have to care for my lethal cancer or care for my crazy wife. If I heard that line in a movie, I'd laugh.

"Nobody's life could be that bad," I'd think.

Bullshit!

I do believe, though, that I'm meant to care for my wife. I know that sounds as if I think God has had a hand in this — as payback for responsibilities I've shirked in the past. Perhaps that's true. I don't know. What I do know is that I have promised to care for Lynne as long as I can.

Can I stay with her until I die? I doubt it. This damn illness will almost certainly strip me of the limited ability I now have to care for myself or my wife. To make matters worse, when things get to that point, I expect Lynne to suffer an attack of mental illness that will force her into a hospital somewhere. My hope is that she will eventually recover. But I'm not sure she will be able to.

EPILOGUE

Who Could've Guessed?

I sometimes think that the only noteworthy thing about my life right now is that I haven't walked into some tavern and started drinking once again. God knows, there are many times when maintained sobriety seems far more senseless than sensible. But I can't face the end of my life and the end of my relationship with my wife drunk and pissing myself and puking and sleeping in alleys and doing all the other things that made my earlier life notable.

So what do I do?

I wake up each morning at about 5:00 a.m. in the apartment Lynne and I have called home for almost 10 years, barely able to move. I walk slowly to the kitchen to switch on the electric coffeemaker, then return to my room to flip on my computer, slip into a pair of slacks, and straighten my bed.

I spend the next hour or so drinking coffee and reading editorials in *The New York Times*, the *Chicago Tribune*, *The Washington Post*, and other newspapers online.

By 6:30, I've dressed myself, shaved, and managed to stuff into place my desperately uncomfortable false teeth. Most mornings I hop into our car and head for a meeting of the fellowship that's held in a former storefront shop about a mile away. I'm in that meeting damn near every morning, unless I have to go to the VA hospital in West Palm Beach for chemotherapy, an exam of some sort, or one of my regular appointments with a kind of mental/emotional advisor or an out-and-out shrink.

I schedule those appointments, if I can, for 8:00 a.m. It's not that I enjoy being in the hospital so much that I can't wait to get there. It's because an early appointment makes it easy for me to find a good parking space. And by making my appointments early, I'm almost certain to be home, and in bed napping or at least resting, by 11:00 a.m. or noon. (My chemo these days is simple. I get one injection into my cancer injection port, located just about three inches beneath my right collarbone. I'm usually done within two hours.)

I hate my appointments. I want to get them over with as soon as is humanly possible. But don't get me wrong. The folks at the VA — including the janitors and coffee shop staff — are some of the nicest men and women I've come across in my life. All of them. My counselor and I hug after every appointment. My shrink and I have enjoyable conversations. My oncologist and I laugh together, talk about books, talk about movies. The chemo nurses are the gentlest, most caring people I've met anywhere. Two of the volunteers in particular — a former cancer patient and his wife — make it clear that they truly want to be where they are, handing out blankets to chemo patients, sometimes books, sometimes snacks. I believe, with my whole mind and heart, that there are no kinder hospital workers or docs or nurses anywhere in the world.

Still, I sure as hell would rather be home having an argument with my wife or stuck in traffic on the interstate or anyplace else you can think of.

Like I said, most of my mornings are spent in the fellowship meetings I've been going to for about 16 years. And while my cancer and treatments aren't a whole hell of a lot of fun, they have gained me — me! — a certain amount of respect, damn near worship, in those meetings. I have a more or less "reserved" seat at a table near the front of the room. Many of the men and women who show up stop to say hello to me, ask how I am. I grab of cup of coffee — oh, yeah, it costs a buck, but that's for unlimited refills — and then sit down.

After the fellowship meeting, I drive a mile or so to a Publix supermarket where I've been a customer for damn near a decade. I never need to buy much, so the visit to the store is more a habit than a requirement. And damn near every employee, from the store's manager to its middle-aged Haitian bagman, treats me with respect. Me! Who could've guessed?

There's a lady in the dairy products section who asks about me and Lynne every time we see each other. An older lady in the bakery section always asks me how I'm doing and almost always has a special piece of cake put aside for me. Employees whose names I don't know ask how I am and smile. The manager goes out of his way to say hello. I should be ashamed to admit this, but the time I spend in that store is one of the high points of my day.

Like they say in the fellowship, I'm just taking it one day at a time… keeping it simple… and trying not to let myself get too hungry, angry, lonely, or tired.

Afterword

By Mark Morgan Ford

Kieran was diagnosed with lung cancer in the spring of 2007. He died on February 6, 2010.

In the 30-odd months in between, we met at The Green Owl dozens of times. I was always a few minutes late. Kieran was always seated at a table in the back, waiting for me when I arrived. He went from there to his AA meeting, which he never missed as far as I know.

We greeted one another with a hug, something we hadn't done prior to his cancer. Kieran and I both came from Irish-American families that frowned on overt affection. Even a man-hug was a stretch for us. For Kieran, I believe the intimacy was a way of saying thanks. For me, it was a bit scary. I could feel how his body was getting smaller.

After the perfunctory what's-doing comments, we settled in to work. Work was talking about his life. I asked questions. He talked. I took notes or ran a recorder, which he could use later on if he needed to.

He didn't like to talk about his cancer, but he did seem to enjoy reminiscing about his life. Part of that enjoyment came, I think, from my listening. His stories were wonderful. And I was transfixed. We talked about everything. His childhood, his schooling, and his stint in the army. His life in Chicago, the move to Florida, and his amazing battle with alcohol. His memory for details was impressive. And he had a natural gift for storytelling that is not uncommon with Irish-Americans.

Sometimes the conversation would drift into philosophical discussions about life and its meaning or the difficulty of marriage, the meaning of friendship, etc. Sometimes he talked to me about Lynne, his fourth wife, with whom he spent almost 18 years.

He told me that Lynne had "saved his life." He was probably right. And if he'd had more time, I know that he would have written much more about her in the book.

Lynne had her own problems. For much of her adult life, she battled mental illness. Even though she was on medication, she was prone to occasional breakdowns, manic behavior that included shopping sprees that they couldn't afford.

And Kieran, as you know from reading his story, was no angel.

They were struggling to pay their rent, and Kieran's capacity to earn money as a freelance writer was quickly diminishing. It wasn't enough that he had to deal with a deadly disease… he had to make money and care for a sometimes-sick wife at the same time.

I offered to help by "lending" him money — enough to take care of his rent and living expenses. He refused at first, but as things got worse, he accepted. He did that only after I promised to repay myself with the proceeds for his autobiography if it ever got published. The rest of the money, he told me, should go to Lynne.

In the beginning, he was able to work on the autobiography for about four hours a day. Later, as the disease progressed, his output decreased considerably. There were days when all he could manage was a few paragraphs. Toward the end, his memory began to fade, so the tape recordings came in handy.

He wrote the first draft in about eight months and then revised it (with some suggestions from me). He also began another ambitious project — a novel meant for adults — which he bravely completed before he died.

As a writer, his strength was in plotting and pace. This made both of his last books easy to read. But although he was unsentimental as a rule, as he got closer to death, his writing became looser in this regard. There was even the occasional bout of purple prose. When I pointed these out to him, he got mad. This was his autobiography, he said, not mine. If he wanted to be sentimental, he damn well could. I left it at that, but noticed that in subsequent drafts the emotion was more restrained.

What is strongest in Kieran's autobiography, I believe, is his voice and the actual stories he told. His voice was hard and efficient — much like Pete Hamill's in *A Drinking Life*. His stories were hard too, and amazing — much like the stories Frank McCourt told in *Angela's Ashes*.

I especially loved listening to his adventures in the military. Not all of them were included in this biography. But some of the best of those left out have been incorporated into his novel, which I'm in the process of editing.

Kieran had a tumultuous family life that left him with considerable regret. He admired his father and was deeply hurt when the man gave up on him. He understood why, and didn't condemn him for it, but it hurt him nonetheless. He had also estranged himself to some degree from his brothers and their children. Worst of all — for him — was that he had all but abandoned his children.

One relationship survived Kieran's drinking intact: his relationship with his mother. During the last two years of his life, he was in constant contact with her. He called her frequently and made trips to visit her whenever he could. Kieran's mother never truly gave up on him, even when he was at his worst. He needed that and appreciated it. He repaid her forgiveness with attention and love.

And, of course, there was Lynne.

Lynne was (and is) a gentle, intelligent, thoughtful person who found in Kieran the man of her dreams. Through it all, she was a devoted spouse. She was a big fan of Kieran's writing and supported his authorial ambitions. "I loved him like no other woman did," she told me. "I made him feel safe and good, and helped him to be well and sober. His own mother grew to love me for that."

I can only imagine the stress that Lynne was under during Kieran's illness. Still, she told me that their last year together was their best. "I took care of him," she said. "I tried, not too successfully, to be a good housewife. (I didn't really enjoy cooking and cleaning.) But I got him fed every day, and I kept him in loving company. We held hands and told each other stories we'd never shared before. Everything on both sides was forgiven."

Kieran worried about how Lynne would fare after he died. (He didn't ask, but he was grateful when I promised to look after her.)

By December of 2009, Kieran could no longer make the trip to The Green Owl. Nor could he attend his beloved AA meetings or writing workshops. I visited him at his home frequently. He was spending most of his time in a bed in the living room, surrounded by books and manuscripts that he read or worked on whenever he had the energy.

The last time I saw him was about a month before he died. He could no longer write but he didn't have to. The two books he had wanted to write had been written.

I asked him how he felt about dying. "I don't like the idea," he said. "But I've loved and been loved. I've done many terrible things but I've also done some good things. I figure I've done more than most people who live 20 years longer than I will."

In February of 2010, Kieran was brought to the Good Samaritan Hospital for treatment. He had been in and out of the hospital several times in the previous few months. At about 6:00 a.m. on Super Bowl Sunday, he died. The hospital staff tried to resuscitate him but without success. They called Lynne immediately, but her phone was on the blink so she didn't receive the message until several hours later.

"It was a sunny morning," she told me. "I was calm, considering. When I got to the parking lot, I was the only person around. It seemed fitting, somehow. They took me to his room. He was behind a curtain, fully dressed. His head was tilted a little towards me, and his eyes were slightly open. He looked as though he were going to speak. I kissed his mouth and held his hand, his cold hand. I sang him a little song that my mom had always told me made her think of me — *You light up my life…* — but I whispered it, so only he would hear.

"I had placed his picture and some candles in my living room — and earlier that day, I was praying there. All of a sudden, I started crying and having deeply sorrowful thoughts of him. Soon, I was sobbing. It was then, I am certain, that Kieran died — that his spirit came to me to say 'Good-bye.' It felt like nothing I'd ever felt before. I am convinced that he was with me."

The memorial service was several days later at St. Andrew's Episcopal Church in Lake Worth. Fr. Paul Rasmus officiated, and the church was full. Kieran's two sons, Dylan and Eamon, were there along with their wives. ("They were shy and so eager to learn more about their dad," Lynne told me.) Kieran's brother Kevin was there, but his brother Pat, who was supposed to speak, didn't show. And there were many of Kieran's friends from AA and his writing group.

This poem was my eulogy:

What can I say, my friend?

That you were selfish and beautiful?

That you were honest to abrasion?

That you died too soon?

What can I write that serves you?

That tells some verity in plain clothes?

It was cold today and windswept

Everything good is swept by

In some far away desert

An ancient figure stands

I am Ozymandious, King of Kings, it says

Look at my fortunes and despair

Nothing matters, it does

This is what we have

The words you have written

The memories that linger